The Basic Ideas
of Occult Wisdom

THE
BASIC
IDEAS
of
OCCULT
WISDOM
Anna Kennedy Winner

*This publication made possible with
the assistance of the Kern Foundation*

**The Theosophical Publishing House
Wheaton, IL U.S.A.
Madras, India/London, England**

Library of Congress Catalog Card No. 75-116528
ISBN: 0-8356-0391-1

Printed in The United States of America

CONTENTS

FOREWORD

The preliminary draft of this book was written in 1942, for the benefit of individual students of this philosophy, with no thought of publication. The writer had already spent many years in study and investigation of these ideas. Now, after a great many more years of study and discussion, this outline is being offered, in a somewhat expanded form, to the reading public, in the belief that it may be of some use. It is an attempt to present the concepts basic to "Occult Wisdom" (considered as a system of philosophy to be investigated and held as a tentative hypothesis rather than as a rigid "belief") in a logical and organized way. For those people who have had some personal experience, or who have some intuitive conviction, which makes them dissatisfied with rigid materialism, it offers a framework of suggested relationships.

During the past decade, the studies of the writer have been focused especially on physical anthropology and the paleontological evidence for human evolution, in the biological sense. If this book should chance to fall into the hands of any anthropologist, the writer hopes that he will remember that it is written primarily for those individuals who cannot intellectually accept the religion they were taught but who feel some emotional craving for, or psychological need for, the "comforts" of religion. It is not intended for those who are in agreement with, and emotionally quite at ease with, statements such as that made by J. Buettner-Janusch in his 1966 book *Origins of Man*, that "of course" man is "nothing but an animal." It is the conviction of the writer that the ideas here presented as basic are not inconsistent with present-day anthropological conclusions as to hominid evolution, and that they may have some heuristic value, even if held only tentatively, for individuals who need some reassurance of a greater life and purpose, in order to have inner stability in their own lives.

Speed reading is not recommended, at least for the first reading, for those to whom these concepts are quite new. The writer has done professional abstract writing for many years, and the material covered here is greatly condensed. To some extent, the phraseology has been simplified, with a view to its effectiveness when read aloud, as for example in a small discussion group of people with similar interests. A pause for thought or discussion at the end of each chapter or two might be useful, to perrit the operation of "reverberating circuits" before adding on more and more new ideas.

The author wishes to thank Harper & Row, Publishers, New York, for permission to include an excerpt from the book *Man in the Modern World,* by Julian Huxley.

CHAPTER I

THE PROBLEM

The most basic idea in our consciousness is our awareness of self. We know we are alive. The one thing we are innately sure of is our own life, which maintains some kind of connection and fundamental unity in spite of the passage of time and all the changes in our bodies brought about by time. We grow up, and we grow older, but all the while we still feel that we are ourselves. We see other people around us, who act more or less as we do when confronted by similar objects, and we extend our knowledge to include the idea that these other people are alive in the same way as ourselves. But we soon see also, as we begin to grow older, that the people around us shift and change, and their number varies. New individuals are born—others who have been alive "die." Even very young children hear of death. Life, then, appears not to be really permanent, although it still feels permanent in our own inner consciousness! In this paradox lies the greatest problem of human life, which seems to demand a solution—yet most people have no idea of where to find the answer, and often feel that there is no answer.

Try as we may to forget it, and to busy ourselves with ordinary activities, or to limit our thinking to the here and now, again and again we are brought face to face with death. Each individual instinctively tries to find, or to form, some acceptable theory as to the meaning of life and death, and, either consciously or unconsciously, seeks for the answer to the great problem: Does death annihilate the conscious self, as well as destroy the body, or is there truth in our inner feeling of the permanence of life? Furthermore, why are we alive in the first place? Where did life come from? What is the meaning of it all?

We talk a great deal in these days about modern scientific knowledge, yet if we ask the scientists about this problem, we always find that they know no more about it than we do ourselves. Scientific knowledge deals with matter and its forms, and the forces or energies which move or change those forms. It knows of consciousness only indirectly, through its instruments or effects. Scientists know nothing directly about the life (or awareness) which is in or behind the forms, and they admit that by their methods they cannot know directly. They may study how consciousness seems to act or react, but this does not tell them what it is, or why. It is not their kind of problem. We must seek elsewhere.

Philosophy supposedly deals with these problems of the meaning of life. But can we find trustworthy answers, or real knowledge, there? We find that there are almost as many systems of philosophy as there are philosophers, and these systems are based upon theories, speculations, hypotheses, worked out by individual thinkers and organized by the power of reason until they seem more or less plausible and acceptable. But what we need is some assurance of truth, not mere theories. It seems that the philosophers cannot offer us any dependable knowledge.

Yet, several thousand years ago there were some philosophers who did not call themselves merely "lovers of wisdom," but rather "knowers"—"Gnostics." What was this knowledge that they had—or thought they had? When we investigate, we find that only fragments of the early writings are left—the rest were either deliberately destroyed or lost. If we delve into these fragments, seeking to reconstruct their system, we find indications that the real Gnosis or "knowledge" was never written down at all, but conveyed by word of mouth, under oath of secrecy, from teachers who were supposed to know to pupils whom they thought worthy. Death was alleged to be the penalty for any betrayal of this secret teaching. So from these writings of the Gnostics we cannot find the answer we seek, but only hints and veiled statements, for which the clues must still be sought elsewhere.

We find that religion attempts to offer answers to all of our philosophical problems. But again we ask: Are the answers true? How do they know? We find many sects or religious organizations, which teach different things, and usually each one claims to have the exclusively correct and true religion. Surely no reasoning mind can accept that sort of claim, if reason is really brought to bear on it. Does one type of religion offer any better proof than another? Some people do not trouble to ask for proof, but are content to accept whatever form of religion was taught to them as children, and to continue to believe in it because some one who claims to be an authority tells them it is true. For them, that is enough, and they feel that the answer to life's problems is known, and all they need to do is to accept the teaching given. This book is not meant for them. But some people are innately sceptical, or have been trained in logic and scientific reasoning, and such people notice inconsistencies, and demand proof, or at least some evidence which fits in with the theories presented. Can the churches offer such evidence? Upon what do they base their ideas?

When we investigate, we find that in the recognized churches, in the Western world, there is no claim at all to direct knowledge, as of the present day. They all refer back to some supposed "authority." If any representative of the churches ever knew, directly and of his own experience, at least we find no one in them now who makes this claim. Jewish teachings are based upon what Christians call the Old Testament. Among Christians, most churches depend upon the books of the Bible (both the Old and the New Testaments) and claim that these books were originally written down under "direct inspiration." But even if, for the moment, we admit that as a hypothetical possibility, still we know that the texts of the books have been copied and rewritten down through the ages, and translated into languages other than the original, and no ordinary person who reads them now can have any assurance that the state-ments in them even give the real thought intended by the original writers. Have we any really logical reason for be-lieving that the preachers or priests give the correct inter-pretation? That would be possible only if they had direct access to some source of knowledge outside of, and more reliable than, the writings themselves. Ever seeking, we find that one man simply quotes another, and he quotes some one a little earlier, or refers once more to the early writings. Where can we find some one who will personally tell us things and in the telling say "These things I know," and give us some guidance as to the course to pursue in order that we may come to know something for ourselves, rather than merely "You must believe it because it is in the Book"?

All through the history of religion in Europe, for nearly twenty centuries, there has been this blind acceptance, on the part of all except individual rebels, of statements based upon authority but offered without any accompanying infor-mation as to how one might verify them for oneself. But European civilization, and European thinking, are after all rather recent in view of the long history of the human race. Even geographically, Europe is but a peninsula of Asia—not really a continent at all, in spite of the fact that European political dominance in recent centuries led the Europeans to think of it as the most important part of the world. There were religions before Christianity—many, many religions. There were great civilizations thousands of years before the Christian era, some of whose very writings are inde-cipherable to us, yet the archeological remains of which show clearly that the people were quite highly developed. These people must have lived and loved and died, even as we do, and they must have faced these same problems of the purpose of life—the enigma of death. Did they find any answer to satisfy their seeking?

Now we come to a very strange thing. So strange is it that most people who have grown up under the influence of modern Western culture never even hear of it. Steeped in the atmosphere of industrial civilization and the urge for material progress, our contemporary writers and their readers are all too apt to think that no one can possibly know the answers to these really important problems of life – that we must just give it up and make the most of what little life we happen to have, and not worry our heads any more than we are obliged to about death, or the real meaning of life on earth. Nobody knows anything about it anyway – why worry? So we think, or at least so speak the unthinking majority. And they act accordingly, carelessly and selfishly, emotionally rather than rationally, each person striving only to achieve what he can for himself or for those few people who happen to be close enough to him to inspire a little unselfish love – or to arouse in him some sense of identification with himself. Those who feel that things ought to be different – who are innately more idealistic – will act less purely for their own immediate benefit and more for the good of mankind. But even they too often do it in a mood of a kind of stoicism, or sometimes desperation, because it is their nature to want to love rather than to hate, and to do good rather than evil, rather than because they really see any logical reason for it. All but a very few, whom we call "mystics," have no idea that there is any way of acquiring real or trustworthy knowledge as to which things are really most important and which actions are really most conducive to inner development, or the welfare of the "soul."

But what do we find when we go back into history, before the Christian era, and study the thought of earlier times? The farther we search, the more generally we find that people believed that there was a knowledge, available for acquisition by the qualified seeker, and really known to some, who were often called "initiates." An ordinary man might not think that he himself could find out all the important knowledge, because it was "occult" or hidden, and given out only to those who prepared to receive it by long and arduous training, for which the ordinary man had no taste or capacity. But he felt perfectly sure that the knowledge existed, and that there were custodians who did possess it, and who could give him valid rules for his own life, on the basis of this knowledge.

How that feeling of certainty was lost is one of the problems of the history of human thinking, and need not concern us now. The thing which interests us is this: people used to feel quite sure that there was a "hidden" or secret inner knowledge, or "Occult Wisdom," and some way of attaining it for those who really sought it long and earnestly enough. Is the knowledge itself lost? Did it really exist at all, as people used to think, or was it only a delusion and a trick of priestcraft? Is there any way by which we, ourselves, can find out whether there really used to be men who were truly "seers" and "knowers"? If there ever was a time when an Inner Wisdom was available, what has happened since then? Is the Wisdom lost, or are there still somewhere those who know, if we could only find them?

Now, it is the conviction of the writer, after approximately fifty years of study and investigation, that the answer to these questions is as follows: There was, and is, an Inner Wisdom. That Wisdom was hidden, or "occult," and its very existence has been largely forgotten or obscured, but it has never been lost. Always it has had its custodians, and still it has them. There is still a way to find them. But that way cannot be trodden by those who are misinformed and unprepared. The higher (or inner) teaching can be given only to those who have certain preliminary qualifications. One of the reasons for this is that "knowledge is power," and the real occult knowledge carries with it power which must not be given to those whose selfishness or immaturity might lead to its misuse. Another, deeper, reason is that the true occult Wisdom is never "given" at all, but won, as a result of independent and self-directed growth in the consciousness of each individual aspirant. The teachers of the race—the custodians of the Wisdom—stand ready to help and guide, and teach, those who have progressed to a certain point. But their consciousness is focused at a higher level than that of normal everyday thinking, and the aspirant must do for himself the preliminary work of raising the level of his own consciousness.

However, an enormous amount of preliminary knowledge (which in former ages was given in the early stages of individual secret teaching) as to the basic ideas of that philosophy here referred to as "Occult Wisdom" is now accessible to the normal consciousness by ordinary methods of study and intellectual research, if we have the right clues to guide us. And the reasonableness and probable validity, as a working hypothesis, of such basic ideas, may be judged by the process of reasoning, without access to any private and secret ("esoteric") teaching or development of ESP or higher-dimensional thinking. Before we can be ready to go ahead into higher levels, we need to read and study, understand and, above all, apply, these basic ideas.

For most students, the first difficulty lies in knowing what and how to study, and how to find the right clues. The word "occultism" is badly misused, and the student who has no trustworthy guide may easily lose himself in a morass of superstition and pseudo-occultism. The word is used here in the technical sense given in the writings of H. P. Blavatsky. "Occult Wisdom" is understood to mean a system of philosophical teachings which in past ages were held in secret by certain advanced thinkers and their accepted pupils. These ideas, according to Madame Blavatsky, were based upon actual investigation and experience, checked and reconfirmed and developed further by successive generations of students, rather than upon mere individual speculation or traditional authority. She said that for many ages the teachings were passed down orally or by actual demonstration, and never committed to writing, except sometimes in a codified or symbolical way. Such writings were not intended to be taken literally, and indeed were full of what she called "blinds" purposely inserted to mislead any possible readers who had not received the more complete secret instruction. In the latter part of the nineteenth century, the custodians of the Wisdom decided that the preliminary teachings could now be made publicly available in books, but the higher or deeper teachings are still reserved for individual aspirants, judged as to their readiness by their individual progress.

At any rate, witchcraft, astrology as commonly understood, crystal balls or Ouija boards, spiritualistic seances, fortune telling, clairvoyant predictions, psychic experiences or visions induced by special methods affecting body chemistry, all have really nothing to do with, and will not lead to, that Wisdom which was once really "occult" or hidden. All so-called psychic phenomena pertain to, or result from contact with, what is called the "astral plane," which is a world dominated by illusion. The aspirant must learn to evaluate such phenomena rather than to value them. The Wisdom is something far higher.

There are now many books available which do contain real clues and much trustworthy information, but the more comprehensive ones are likely to be very abstruse, while some are couched in figurative or symbolical language. The task of reading them all (or even a considerable proportion of them), and correlating and checking and winnowing out those nuggets of wisdom, is far too time-consuming for most people to undertake. The supposedly simple and introductory books so far available seem each to present the point of view of a single individual or sect, or to deal with some one special aspect, rather than to present the truly basic ideas of the whole philosophy in an organized way.

The present writer, after many years of intensive focusing on this particular line of research, reading in theosophy, mysticism, Oriental religions, parapsychology, and other related fields, as well as having contact with and consultation with other students who seemed to be further advanced in their understanding, became convinced that the fundamental or basic ideas of the formerly secret teaching here called occultism could be conveyed in a relatively small book, simply written. For some individuals, the material presented here may serve as an introduction to this line of thought, and for those who have already read more widely it may serve as a framework and aid to clarification and organization of ideas.

If the reader grasps the fundamental unity of the scheme, after examining this outline, then perhaps it would be well to hold it in mind for some years, checking with other study and experience, and perhaps rereading at a later date, before forming any opinion as to its probability of truth.

CHAPTER II

LINES OF INVESTIGATION

In ancient days, as already indicated, people used to believe that there was a knowledge, or Wisdom, which was never revealed fully to ordinary men, but which was available to specially prepared and trained aspirants or candidates who might eventually become "initiated" into the "mysteries." It was thought that this knowledge included a full explanation of the meaning and purpose of life (from which valid rules for behavior could be derived) and information about death and the condition of the "dead," as well as the story of the beginning of the world, and instructions about the "gods" or forces of nature.

In our Western civilization, at the present time, this type of knowledge seems to be lost, if, indeed, it was knowledge rather than delusion. People construct theories, or refer back to the supposed authority of ancient scriptures, but most people no longer believe that there is any way of obtaining real information on these points. For an earnest student, however, it is hard to believe that if such knowledge ever existed, it could have been completely lost. Is there any method by which, at the present time, we can reconstruct the outline, at least, of this Ancient Wisdom?

There are several methods, none of them completely satisfactory in itself, but which we can use in conjunction with each other.

In the first place, there is the method of the study of comparative religion. All of the great religions claim to have been founded by some great Teacher who *knew*. If there was any basis at all for this claim, even in a limited sense, the background of knowledge must have been the same in all cases, however much the external presentation of the truth may have varied, in being adapted to peoples of different traditions and different stages of development. Religions vary a great deal, superficially. But truth, or the reality of the whole universe, is outside of space and time and thus no presentation of it in the language of the ordinary three-dimensional world can be really accurate or complete. Different presentations may look or sound very different, being based on different sides or aspects of the whole, yet in itself, the whole truth must be one and the same. If we examine carefully the great religions of the past, in each case going back as much as possible to the original teaching, before it became overlaid with the later accumulations of the misinterpretations of lesser minds, tradition, superstition, and the contrivances of priestcraft, we shall find that we can pick out certain basic ideas which are common to them all. And we may perhaps conclude that these formed part of some real knowledge behind them all.

The second method is the study of the experiences and statements of those lesser but still unusual people, a few in each century down through the ages, who have spoken of some direct access to truth which they themselves claimed to have attained. Such people are usually called mystics. In this case, again, we find a great variety of detail in the statements, but again, when we study them closely, we shall find a residue which is common to all. Is it not possible that these people did obtain, through some methods not yet available to, or never used by, the average person, glimpses of an inner truth? Being imperfect, and untrained (because for nearly two thousand years, in the West at least, there have been no regular schools of the "mysteries" where those interested could go for systematic and definite training of their unusual faculties), these people saw things confusedly, and naturally interpreted them in conformity with the tradition and superstitions current in the period or culture in which they lived. But if, in spite of all of the confusion, we find that there are statements on which they all agree, may we not at least tentatively form the hypothesis that these things also may be part of the truth we are seeking? If it were all delusion and imagination, would we find these basic agreements?

In ordinary science, if we find that the independent testimony of a number of different investigators agrees upon certain points, even though we may not be qualified to check the investigations for ourselves, do we not assume that the scientists have obtained some real knowledge? The great mystics have usually been men (or women) of considerable nobility of life and purity of character, as well as apparent probity and sincerity, and their inner illumination has often seemed to give them some peculiar quality which made their contemporaries look upon them as supernormal. Therefore it would seem that a really impartial investigation and search for truth should take into consideration their testimony, however strange it may seem at first to the ordinary practical mind. Aldous Huxley used the term "the perennial philosophy" for the concepts he personally distilled from some of these lines of investigation.

Some support for our hypotheses may be found in the researches of modern science. It is true that scientific facts alone will never suffice to give a complete idea of the world and the meaning of life and death, but every scientific fact, if it is a fact, must be part of the great whole we are seeking to understand, and no religious or philosophical theory could be accepted as true (by a truly careful seeker) if it did not find a place for those parts of the truth ascertainable by scientific methods. We have no room here to go into detail about many of the discoveries of science which bear some relation to occult knowledge, but some suggestions may be made, and the reader will be able to work out other ideas for himself.

One of the most important discoveries of science, from the point of view of its relation to the occult knowledge to which we are seeking clues, is that "matter" is an illusory concept. Apparently solid matter is not really solid at all. When a substance is divided and redivided you come, not to a solid indivisible building brick as the ancients used to think (which was why they called it "atom" or uncuttable), but to a system of energy pulsations or vortices. We use words such as protons and electrons, mesons and neutrons, and the physicists are continually busy investigating and rearranging their ideas on the subject. The only thing we are sure of is that the "ultimate particles" are not matter, in the old sense of the word, but energy, and it is only some relationship or structural arrangement of these units of energy which serves to build up the structure we call matter. Furthermore, we find that all the infinite variety of substances in the known universe seems to be built up, by variations in number and arrangement, of these same identical units of energy. A hundred years ago, a man of science would have scoffed incredulously at the occult statement that the worlds are all formed from one primary stuff, which is not matter at all, but a manifestation of the one divine life, but now we find many of the foremost scientists reaching conclusions which sound very much like that.

Turning to the science of psychology, we find that man's conscious mind is only a partial or surface presentation of some fundamental self which includes the memory of everything which has ever occurred to him, even in infancy. And the researches of men such as Jung indicate that in dreams there is a form of symbolism which is shared by different men, and which to some thinkers suggests the existence of a "collective unconscious" in which individuals share in some fundamental unity.

In another direction, we find that the various societies for psychical research have built up such a vast literature of authenticated case histories as to make it impossible for an unprejudiced mind to deny the factual occurrence of many phenomena formerly classed as superstition. For example, some people undoubtedly have had visions of future events. And innumerable cases have occurred where the image or vision of a man who was dying or in danger in one part of the world has been seen, and perhaps a message received, by some member of his family or friend far away, and later checking has confirmed that the time was the same, or the message correct. Most of the cases recorded by psychical research societies deal with vision or apparent transference of thought which seems to be sporadic or accidental. But the subject has been approached from a different angle by investigators of what is called ESP, or extrasensory perception, in experiments where the conditions have been carefully arranged and controlled in advance – and the number of successes seems to indicate the possibility that there is some method of perceiving, or receiving mental impressions, which does not depend upon the ordinary channels of the five senses.

This is more plausible and credible to us in these days than it could ever have been to our great-grandparents, because we are familiar every day with the phenomena of broadcasting, and know, beyond the shadow of a doubt, that the air around us is filled at all times with vibrations which we do not and cannot perceive until we have a properly constructed and properly tuned receiving set. We know also that these vibrations travel with the speed of light, and as long ago as World War II, we became quite accustomed to tuning in on our radio set to a "news round-up" in which we would hear three or four different voices reporting from different parts of the world, with no perceptible interval to correspond to the great distances involved. Thus when we find that occultists tell us that it is possible for a man, who has already acquired certain preliminary qualities, to construct a sort of receiving set in his own brain, by the activation of organs which are ordinarily not in operation, and then to receive communications from the mind of some one similarly developed on the other side of the world, and to feel as close a sense of contact as we do when we talk over the telephone, we find that, even if the statement is new to us, it is hard to deny that it might possibly be true.

In the literature of occultism, there are many books which, it is claimed, have been written as a result of some such telepathic communication. While it would be unwise to accept such a claim without some supporting evidence, it is interesting to compare the statements made in these different books, and to note the ways in which their teachings correspond.

Madame Helena Petrovna Blavatsky, who founded The Theosophical Society in 1875, said that she had spent some years in Tibet in personal contact with several highly advanced occult teachers who were able to keep in touch with her later by transmission of thought. She claimed to have received, by some telepathic means, much of the material written in her books. But she also indicated the possibility of mistakes due to imperfect transmission, and said that some statements were "blinds." She always stressed her human susceptibility to human fallibility in the role of "messenger," and never intended her writings to be taken as authoritative. Nevertheless, the works of H. P. B. (as her students called her), particularly *The Secret Doctrine,* contain such a tremendous amount of material, impressively presented, that they are the primary source of much of the literature of The Theosophical Society, and of various groups which split off from that society but still belong to what is known as the Theosophical Movement. This literature also forms the basis for much of the teachings of the several varieties of modern Rosicrucianism and of many other groups which claim to have secret or occult teachings. Many pseudo-occult organizations utilize the ideas obtained from the works of Madame Blavatsky, without giving her (or her teachers) any credit for them, but adding all kinds of nonsense and misinterpretations.

The present survey is not in any sense all-inclusive, and ideas from various sources have been correlated. The statements made are not intended to be taken as dogma. The Buddha himself taught that one should not believe in a thing merely because it is said, or handed down in tradition, or written by a supposed sage, or supposed to have been inspired, or even because he himself said it, but rather to believe only when the doctrine, writing, or saying is corroborated by one's own reason and consciousness.

What is offered is a much condensed synthesis, an attempt to provide, in an organized form, a framework on which to fit ideas and experiences from other sources, and to restate in a logical relationship what the writer believes to be the fundamental or basic ideas of that hidden Wisdom which has seemed for so long to be lost or unreal. The reader should not expect to find here any "secret" teachings of the Wisdom itself, but only a presentation of ideas corresponding to the early or preliminary teaching which used to be given privately to admitted candidates. In some cases, a brief account is also given of some supplementary ideas which the reader may encounter in other books claiming to deal with this subject. The Wisdom itself still remains accessible only to those who have developed themselves to the necessary point, but this may help to provide a few preliminary guidelines.

CHAPTER III

THE BASIC IDEA OF ONE LIFE IN ALL THINGS

The very first fundamental idea of occultism is that everything in the universe is One. There is no way in which any mind, or body, or photon or electron, could exist without, or outside of, that One Life.

The Christian religion speaks of One God, but for many Christians the concept of "God" does not really correspond to this idea of the One. Traditional Christianity is still deeply impregnated with ideas derived from the ancient Jewish scriptures, in which the concept of God was distinctly anthropomorphic. Many people who have been subjected to orthodox religious instruction think of God as "personal," a being with many human qualities, who created the universe as something distinct from himself, as a man might make a machine, and then set it going—and who intervenes in its operations, sometimes, arbitrarily, producing "miracles" which are contrary to the "laws of Nature." The occult concept is distinctly not that of a "personal God."

The One has no qualities which can be expressed in words, being beyond the separative faculty of mind which describes things according to their qualities. Our minds are so limited and finite that no statement which we could make about It could possibly be accurate. We find writers using such terms as the One Unknowable, the First Cause, the Infinite All. In *The Secret Doctrine,* H. P. Blavatsky gives as the first of three fundamental principles of the doctrine: "An Omnipresent, Eternal, Boundless and Immutable Principle, on which all speculation is impossible, since it transcends the power of human conception and can only be dwarfed by any human expression or similitude. It is beyond the range and reach of thought."

In Ancient Egypt, the common people worshipped many gods, most of them in strange forms, partly animal and partly man. But there is evidence that the truly initiated priesthood never believed in these many gods, except as symbolical expressions of various aspects or qualities which the divine might be presumed to have when in manifestation. They believed that the truth was too high to be understood by the uneducated, and thus the outer gods were set before the people to be worshipped. But the priests themselves, if they were of high enough rank to be instructed in the mysteries, honored the One.

In the religious traditions of India, more of the really ancient and formerly esoteric or secret teachings have been preserved in the ancient scriptures written in Sanskrit than in any other supposedly sacred writings. The Vedas, of which the Upanishads are a part, were really "occult," passed on only orally to selected students, for many centuries before being written down. As part of the *Mahabharata,* the great epic poem in Sanskrit which was also accumulated orally over a long period, we have what is perhaps the most wonderful piece of religious writing which has been preserved for us – the *Bhagavad-Gita.* In trying to explain what an occultist means by the One Life which is in all things, some quotations from the *Gita* may be helpful.

In the second discourse, the Lord Krishna, a manifestation of "the One" who is supposed to be speaking to the warrior Arjuna, says: "Know THAT to be indestructible by whom all this is pervaded." In the seventh discourse, we find: "Know this to be the womb of all beings. I am the source of the forth-going of the whole universe and likewise the place of its dissolving." Also: "Those devoid of Reason think of Me, the unmanifest, as having manifestation, knowing not my supreme nature. . . . I know the beings that are past, that are present, that are to come, O Arjuna, but no one knoweth Me." In the sixth discourse, we find: "By Me all this world is pervaded in my unmanifested aspect; all beings have root in Me, I am not rooted in them."

And the tenth discourse says: "I am the Self, seated in the heart of all beings: I am the beginning, the middle, and also the end of all beings. . . . And whatsoever is the seed of all beings, that am I, O Arjuna; nor is there aught, moving or unmoving, that may exist bereft of Me. There is no end of My divine powers. . . . Whatsoever is glorious, good, beautiful, and mighty, understand thou that to go forth from a fragment of My splendor. But what is the knowledge of all these details to thee, O Arjuna? Having pervaded this whole universe with one fragment of Myself, I remain."

This last statement is perhaps the supreme expression of the idea. There is One Life in all beings – men, animals, plants, the very atoms themselves, and the "empty space" between the atoms – even in the farthest galaxy of fiery suns that we can imagine. And yet this is not a mere pantheism, or concept of a divine life in Nature, because beyond all the manifestations of the universe, which are pervaded by one "fragment," THAT still remains.

Yet, when we investigate the writings of the mystics, in all religions, we find them speaking of some experience by which the individual feels himself "one with the One." This Divine Self, which is in the universe, and beyond the universe, is in some mysterious way felt to have a fundamental identity with man's own inner being. This is the essence of the mystic experience. The self of man is part of the great Self, and is felt to be essentially identical with it and, potentially at least, equally infinite. The old Sanskrit saying *"tat tvam asi"* means "Thou art THAT."

Again quoting the *Bhagavad-Gita*, we find that the sixth discourse says: "The self, harmonized by yoga, seeth the Self abiding in all beings, all beings in the Self; everywhere he seeth the same. He who seeth Me everywhere, and seeth everything in Me, of him will I never lose hold, and he shall never lose hold of Me."

In later chapters we shall discuss the question of the goal of life and the meaning of the term "yoga" used in this quotation. For the present, our aim is simply to indicate the general belief, held by the mystics of all ages, that there is a supreme Self with which the individual aspires to realize his unity, which is immanent in all the manifested universe of matter and yet which transcends it.

This idea of the One Life, which runs counter to the assumptions of crude materialism, means that there is no such thing as "lifeless" matter. Matter and spirit are two aspects of manifestation, and in a manifested universe, neither one can exist without the other. The forms of matter which seem to us lifeless are simply those forms in which the vibrations produced by mind or spirit are too subtle to be perceived by the physical senses. It is not within the province of science, as science, to discuss this proposition, but we find that many great men of science, speaking personally, express themselves similarly. For example, the eminent biologist Julian Huxley, in his essay "Philosophy in a World at War," rejects the idea of the "apparent dualism" between matter and spirit, or mind. He says: "The only logical alternative to dualism is monism—that matter and mind are two aspects of one reality, that there exists one world-stuff, which reveals material or mental properties according to the point of view. Looked at from the outside, the world-stuff has nothing but material properties; its operations appear as mind to itself, from within.... But if the world-stuff is both matter and mind in one; if there is no break in continuity between the thinking, feeling adult human being and the inert ovum from which he developed; no break in continuity between man and his remote pre-amoebic ancestor; no break in continuity between life and not-life—why, then, mind or something of the same nature as mind must exist throughout the entire universe. This is, I believe, the truth."

The occult teaching, at any rate, is that even in minerals there is a kind of "life," although it is beyond our powers of conception. In the plant kingdom we find life that we call by that name, with sensitivity to light and warmth, and to moisture and pressure, and capacity for reaction to stimuli. The life in animals we of course recognize as similar to our own, except that there is apparently a lack of self-consciousness as well as of the capacity for abstract or symbolical thought. Life is thought of here not as a phenomenon dependent upon protoplasm, with the capacity for physical growth and self-reproduction as its main characteristic. Rather, life is synonymous with awareness. There is a single, unitary, all-pervading life and awareness immanent in the universe as a whole, which also transcends all manifestation and is "the Unknowable" to us, but in which and by which we are known. To use another terminology, God is in us, and we are in Him, "from Everlasting to Everlasting."

Some people believe that there is a great gap between human life and the life of that which they call God, with no lives which show any intermediate stages of development. But we find in other respects that nature makes no sudden leaps, but everywhere progresses by gradual development, each stage merging into the one above. May we not therefore, by analogy, conclude that there are kingdoms of life above the human, just as the life of the plant and animal kingdoms is below it? Because "the One" is supreme, does it necessarily follow that there can be no lesser beings who are higher than man? When once more we go back to the concepts of the most ancient religions, we find everywhere the assumption that there existed a whole host of lesser lives, thought of as part of the divine Whole, but thought of also as possessing distinct attributes, with powers and capacities greater than, or different from, those of human beings. Such were the "gods" or forces of nature. Even in the Christian religion, we hear of angels and archangels, and in the folklore of all peoples, whether Christian or pagan, we hear of those lesser powers of nature called sometimes fairies, sometimes sprites or elves or mermaids, sometimes (in the Sanskrit) *devas*. If there were no basis at all for such beliefs, how is it that they have always been so widespread? These ideas have been held not only by primitive and ignorant people, but those forerunners of modern science, the medieval alchemists, who were highly intelligent men (and whose terminology is now recognized to have been symbolical or "veiled"), spoke often of all sorts of non-human but nevertheless animate forces, which seem strangely akin to the "nature spirits" and "gods" of the older religions.

All of this sounds very strange to the modern Occidental mind. But just as occultists assert that there is One Life in the universe, so also they assert that there are minor lives at many different levels of development, of which ordinary human beings know nothing, because we are not "tuned in" to them, but which form part of the great scheme. After all, ordinary human beings possess only five senses, through which to receive impressions of the universe, and we know, for instance, how very small is the range of human sensitivity to light waves. Have we any right, therefore, to assume that the things which we do not know cannot exist? Do we "contact" all of the universe?

One particular part of the occult concept which may be worth mentioning here is that, while the One Unmanifested is in and beyond the universe as a whole, in our own solar system there is also a very special form of life centered in the sun. We know that the physical sun is the life-giver of the system, and that without its energy nothing could live. We know that the sun influences us not only by light and heat, but by a great range of electromagnetic forces, and that when there is an especially strong disturbance on the surface of the sun, visible to us in the form of sunspots, there is likely to be also a disturbance of broadcast communications. Occultists hold that there are also more subtle forms of influence radiating from the sun, which interpenetrate us and affect our lives in every way, and that the solar system as a whole may be thought of as one Great Life, "in Whom we live and move and have our being." In occult literature we shall find this great being usually referred to as the "Solar Logos."

CHAPTER IV

THE BASIC IDEA OF THE DIFFERENT STATES OF MATTER

We are all familiar with the fact that physical matter may exist in different states, as solid, liquid, or gas. In chemistry we find a different classification, according to which substances are analyzed as to the elements of which they are composed. These chemical elements, for many years, were thought by scientists to be the ultimate building bricks of the universe. But research by nuclear physicists into the structure of the atom has given a very different picture of things.

The scientific finding which is most at variance with the common sense impression is that there is no such thing as solid matter. In fact, there really isn't any "matter" at all, in the old sense of the word, but only structured energy.

Let us analyze this statement. All ordinary matter is composed of molecules, and these molecules are made up of structured groups of atoms. When the atom itself is examined, we find it to be described by some writers (attempting to give a conceivable mental picture instead of a mere mathematical indication) as a miniature solar system, with a complex central core or nucleus, bearing, for each chemical element, a certain number of positive electrical charges, and, outside of the nucleus, a varying number of electrons, each bearing a unit negative charge. The electrons are spoken of as moving in orbits around the center, very much as the planets move in orbits around the sun. The atom is not "solid," but, in proportion to their size, or rather "mass," the electrons are just as far away from their center as the planets of the solar system are away from the central sun. So there is a great deal of empty space in ordinary "solid" matter.

We are told by the astrophysicists that there are some stars in which the atoms have been shorn of some or most of their outer electrons, and the central nuclei are packed together in a way which produces matter of a density almost inconceivably greater than that of any matter known on earth. Yet those nuclei, in themselves, are only collections of electrical charges, operating in some way to produce a tension which we call "mass."

We find in the Hindu scriptures that matter is referred to as "illusion," or, in the Sanskrit, "maya," and instead of turning away in disgust from idle metaphysical imaginings, it is now (as contrasted with a century ago) scientifically permissible to wonder whether those old writers did not have some understanding of something which our modern scientists are just beginning to glimpse.

What did the ancients teach about the structure of the world? We are familiar with the statement, repeated rather scornfully in some textbooks, that the Greek philosophers thought all matter was composed of four elements: earth, air, fire, and water. But did they use those words in the ordinary sense? The Greeks were very subtle thinkers, and many of their philosophers, particularly if they had studied in some mystery school, or were pupils of men who had, may have used words with a symbolical or mystical meaning. Many of the greatest had studied in Egypt, and although at that time Egypt had already fallen far below the wisdom of the time of its ancient glories, nevertheless, some fragments of the original wisdom teaching may have been still accessible in the temples.

At the present time, we have available a great mass of literary material from Egypt, and when we study it we find that the ancient Egyptians believed very firmly in a universe composed of matter of different grades or densities. They thought that, in addition to the physical body, every man possessed a number of bodies of more subtle material, corresponding to various subtle worlds. These subtle bodies, the "ka" and the "ba" and others whose names we need not list, withdrew from the physical body at death, and the man's essential self lived on in them. Often at the end of a burial chamber there was a painted door, and the dead man in his subtle bodies was supposed to come through that painted door to enjoy the pictures and offerings which had been placed in the tomb. If we believe that matter is solid, obviously such stories are mere idle superstition. But when we remember how large a proportion of empty space exists even in the densest stone, we may perhaps conceive of the possibility of a body of some finer substance which would have no more difficulty in passing through stone than sunlight has in passing through glass.

When we examine the great religions of ancient India, Hinduism and Buddhism, we find again this belief in many superphysical worlds, each finer than, and interpenetrating, the one "below" it. Again we find the "elements," but here we find the explanation to correspond with the names. "Earth" is our ordinary physical world, speaking metaphorically or occultly. "Water" is the next higher world, the world of emotions, or *kama* (the Sanskrit word for desire.). Above water is the region of "air," or mind; above that "fire," or intuition; and above that "ether," or spirit. This composes the "five worlds" sometimes spoken of as if their total made up the universe. But we find that above these five, in some writings, two others are listed, making a total of seven.

Christians sometimes speak of the "seventh heaven," and the Moslem tradition includes this idea, as does the Zoroastrian. We find indications that the Egyptians really believed in a sevenfold universe. All of these similar traditions indicate some basic idea shared by them all. The great nineteenth century writer on occultism, H. P. Blavatsky, in her monumental work *The Secret Doctrine,* has gone into the discussion of these matters at great length, citing innumberable quotations from all sorts of ancient scriptures in support of her thesis that there are seven "planes" of matter. The reader who is interested in the accumulation of evidence is hereby referred to her writings, but here we have room only for a summary.

Using the Sanskrit terminology, the highest "plane" (in some writings) is called Adi, which merely means "first." This is "matter," in the sense of a vehicle for spirit, in a state inconceivably fine. Blavatsky speaks, metaphorically, of the first tiny bubbles or "holes in space" produced by the outpouring of the divine breath when bringing the universe into manifestation. Then somehow the smallest units at this level (for which she uses the term "atoms," but indicates that this means something quite different from the atoms of physical science) combine to produce the units which in turn make up the "matter" of the plane next below, Anupadaka. This name means "parentless." Next comes the plane of Atma, sometimes referred to as the "spiritual" plane (both Atma and spirit have the root meaning of "breath"); then that of Buddhi, or the "intuitional"; then that of Manas, or the plane of mind; then that of Kama (desire), called also the astral or emotional plane; and finally the seventh and lowest, the ordinary physical plane. The word "astral," meaning "starry," seems to have been invented by medieval mystics who perceived some shining world beyond the physical, and the word is generally the one used in modern occult terminology. (But Blavatsky uses the word "astral" where more modern authors usually write "etheric.")

Now we must understand what is meant by the word "plane." This term is widely used by English-speaking writers on occult subjects, but it is actually most misleading. In ordinary English, a plane is a flat two-dimensional surface, but in occult terminology, the physical "plane" is our ordinary three-dimensional world, the astral "plane" has four dimensions, the mental "plane" has five dimensions, and so on up. Or so the scheme is presented in some books, in what is no doubt a much too literal-minded way.

At any rate, the concept we are asked to form is that of many worlds, of successively finer grades or types of substance (although only the lowest or densest is perceptible to our five senses as what we call "matter"), each interpenetrating and extending beyond the one denser than itself.

Around our physical earth, the astral and mental "planes" may be thought of more as globes than planes, each permeating the interstices of the space occupied by the dense globe of our planet, but also extending beyond its atmosphere farther out into space. This does not take into account the supposed extension into higher dimensions, which our ordinary minds cannot picture in any way.

We are told that every human body, besides the dense physical core which we see, has in it and around it a number of interpenetrating sheaths (sheath in the sense of container, as a possible container of the spirit), each made up of the material of one of these more subtle worlds. They are sometimes called "vehicles," instead of "sheaths," or sometimes merely "finer bodies." ("Finer" here is used to mean made up of more minute particles.)

In various books on occultism, we find two "bodies" listed for the physical plane of matter, instead of only one. We are told that besides the visible dense body, every man has an "etheric" or "vital" sheath or body, which is physical in the sense of belonging to the physical plane, and in being discarded at death, but which is invisible to ordinary sight, because it is made up of "matter" of the finest or "etheric" subdivisions of the physical plane—finer than ordinary gases. We are told that this is not a real vehicle for experience, but a kind of "force field" which forms the matrix or energy pattern upon which the dense physical form is built up—or repaired in case of injury—and that it is also the conveyor of vitality and of sensation. That is, that the dense body has no capacity for sensation in itself, but that we "feel" only when the vital etheric currents run along the nerve channels.

Under anesthesia, we are told, this etheric network is displaced, only partially under local anesthesia, but completely separated from the body under total anesthesia, though still connected to the brain through the top of the head by a sort of shining cord, which some clairvoyants claim to be able to see. The occult teaching is that it is this displacement which is really responsible for the lack of sensitivity. But at death "the silver cord is loosed" and the connection is permanently broken, so that the dense body is no longer organized and capable of functioning as a unit, but breaks up into separate groups of cells which gradually disintegrate. In life, the "etheric" or "vital" body is supposed to project about half an inch beyond the surface of the dense body, and to show, to clairvoyant sight, lines of force or radiation, which will be shining in a healthy person, but grayish and drooping in one who is ill. The finer or higher sheaths are said to be more or less ovoid in shape, extending a foot or more from the body and forming the "aura."

What is sometimes called "ectoplasm" is thought to be made up of an extrusion of part of the field of force of the "etheric" body. Its occasional visibility might be explained by its having gathered around itself fine particles of dust or moisture from the atmosphere, as the track of an electron is made visible in a cloud chamber. Or it may draw some other material from a medium's body. At any rate, the production of "ectoplasm" is an abnormal and disruptive phenomenon, which causes a damaging drain on the vital force of the individual from whom it is produced.

The astral and mental bodies are said to have in them certain centers or vortices of force which act somehow as the equivalent of "sense organs" for those bodies. In Sanskrit the term for such a center is *chakra,* which literally means "wheel." In many books, we find that the chakras are said to correspond, in their location, to the endocrine glands of the physical body. There are many pseudo-occult publications which go into great detail about the so-called development of the chakras, but valid information on the subject is really "occult," because of the danger of unsupervised experimentation. That is, the organization and development of the centers or chakras of the finer bodies is part of the subject matter of real occult study.

These centers receive impressions from the worlds of finer matter to which they correspond, but the impressions are confused until the individual has acquired training and experience, just as the impressions given by sight are confused to a new-born baby or a man whose sight has been restored after blindness. But in the case of the chakras, the technique for bringing these impressions into the waking consciousness, by linking them up somehow to the physical brain, requires occult training, if one is to avoid the danger of a kind of electrical shock which could cause mental aberration or even complete insanity. Some of the best books say that no individual should ever undertake to "open up" the chakras or try to link them unless he can be constantly watched, during the process, by a highly advanced guru who is completely clairvoyant. Such a guru could observe the motions of the subtle forces involved, and thus put an immediate stop to the attempt if something starts to go in a wrong way. Otherwise, one may quite literally blow out one's mind. Therefore, it is highly dangerous to try to put into practice any merely printed instructions.

The essential idea (apart from all such details) is merely that each individual possesses, in addition to the physical body, these several finer bodies or sheaths, made up of matter of the planes of finer substance which interpenetrate the matter of the world known to physical science.

These occult concepts may seem quite fantastic at first, but perhaps the reader may consider them tentatively as hypotheses, pending further study. Probably the statements about the seven planes should not be taken too literally, but they may offer a framework for thinking, in order to account for various psychic phenomena and mystical experiences. At present, our senses are limited, and the theories of orthodox physical science are almost as limited, and do not seem able to account for such phenomena.

CHAPTER V

THE BASIC IDEA OF PROGRESSIVE DEVELOPMENT

The idea of progressive development is one of the most important concepts of occultism. Otherwise stated, all true occultists are essentially evolutionists. But they believe not only in the evolution of form, which is taught in modern biology, but also in the evolution of the life within the form—the evolution of consciousness itself.

The idea that there is a real progress in nature is relatively new to ordinary thinking. In many cultures, people have looked to the past for a "Golden Age," or believed that there is "nothing new under the sun," and that everything goes around and around in endless cycles of repetition.

The modern idea of progress arose only a few hundred years ago, and flowered especially in the nineteenth century, when most scientists were still deists, but it is questioned now by those who consistently adopt what Gerald Heard has called the "mechanomorphic" conception of the universe. However, many advanced scientists, particularly those who are specialists in biological evolution, now agree that the actual facts prove that evolutionary progress has occurred. In spite of the deployment of living forms into all possible environments, and the fact that some forms have ceased to evolve or have degenerated, there has been a persisting tendency, throughout the successive ages of earth history, for the vanguard of life to occupy forms with increasingly complex nervous systems, capable of increasing sensitivity and intelligence.

In his book *Evolution in Action*, Julian Huxley has a chapter on "The path of biological progress," which he defines as "improvement which permits or facilitates further improvement." He states that biological progress has demonstrably occurred and that it "is marked by the intensification and improvement of mental capacity and its results." From this he develops the idea of a "morality of evolutionary direction," according to which "anything which permits or promotes open development is right, anything which restricts or frustrates development is wrong." Various other contemporary writers have spoken of a trend toward "growth of awareness" or "expansion of consciousness" as having marked the evolution of life on earth so far, and they have utilized this concept as an indication of the proper direction for mankind. It is possible, on the basis of this completely scientific concept, to construct an ideal for a future human progress which would be both natural and ethical. But the concept gains in richness and depth of meaning, and particularly in emotional appeal, if it is looked at from the occult point of view, with reincarnation as the method by which such growth or expansion of consciousness can be envisaged for the individual, not merely for the species.

In some modern occult writings, we find the word "involution" used almost as much as "evolution," and we need to understand the concept embodied in the word. In conformity with the idea of matter, or substance, in seven different levels or degrees of fineness, or seven states or planes, as outlined in the previous chapter, it is thought that the divine spirit, in coming into manifestation, must "involve" itself in successively denser states of matter, descending from the highest plane gradually lower and lower until it reaches the mineral kingdom of the physical plane, before the life essence thus involved can begin to evolve upward through the kingdoms of nature as we know them, thence to continue its evolution in superphysical realms.

When manifestation begins, and the process of densification of matter leads to the formation of the different planes and then the growth in complexity of material forms, this spirit, which we have called the One Life, is thought to obtain (at the same time) a kind of richness and enjoyment of self-fulfillment by creating different projections of itself. These projections of the spirit differentiate further as they become more and more involved downwards in matter and then evolve upwards as apparently separate existences, meeting with diverse experiences in those existences. Thus there is in some sense an "increase of awareness" even for the divine awareness.

In his book *Creative Evolution,* the philosopher Bergson contended that the theories of random variation due to mutation, and natural selection of those forms which varied most successfully, hardly seemed adequate to account for the infinite complexities and harmony of development which we find everywhere in nature. Of course, he was writing before the formulation of the modern synthetic theory of evolution, which is more adequate than the theories of his day. He concluded that there must be an *élan vital* or vital urge which operated to cause evolution in the direction of some goal or purpose, and that mutations which led to progressive evolution were not merely lucky accidents, but the result of an inner life force pressing forward in the effort to function in some better way. There is no valid evidence for this, from the point of view of merely physical science, but it is an incontrovertible fact that there has constantly been a progressive trend.

To understand the occultist's point of view, we need to add to Bergson's theorizing the idea that the inner consciousness itself, which is a faint shadowing of the divine consciousness, is growing and developing all the while, as the outer forms develop. The forms are merely vehicles for the spirit within, and they are used just so long as they enable that spirit to learn new lessons, and discarded for new and better forms when they become too crystallized and limited.

Let us look at the evolution of animal forms on earth from this point of view. At one time there were no forms more highly developed than the amphibians. Later came the age of the dominance of the great reptiles – the dinosaurs and their relatives – and then after a long period had passed, the dinosaurs had all become extinct, and the "age of mammals" was going on. There was no loss of "life," the occultist might say; the life which was in the great dinosaurs was the same life which came back later on in the forms of the mammals, because the time had come for new and different experiences. When a species becomes extinct, it is the form which has failed to adapt itself to changed conditions, but the life returns in different, better forms. Thus, for example, at the present time, we find that many species of large mammals have become extinct or in danger of extinction, but animals domesticated by man are increasing. Time was when great wolf packs roamed over regions now "civilized" and free from wolves. But in those civilized communities we now find dogs, and the inner consciousness in dog forms, an occultist would say, is that which was formerly in the wolves, now learning lessons of loyalty and service and devotion which will never be lost, but which will find a higher type of bodily expression in some future aeon.

In regard to the evolution of the human spirit, traditional Christianity seems to believe that it is possible for a human being to become spiritually perfect (that is, fit for "heaven") by some magic rite of baptism, or, in some sects, by "confession" or "repentance" and the declaration of belief in some particular formula. None of the older Oriental religions has ever believed in any such sudden change to perfection. It is contrary to all reason and logic. Everywhere else in our experience, we find that growth is a process, and to get from one stage to another one must pass through all the intervening stages. You may go slower or faster, but the distance must be traversed. We see this even in the matter of physical distance. You may travel from one place to another on foot, by horse, by train or motor vehicle, or by air, and in each case, by using improved methods, you may decrease the time consumed. But you cannot, in a three-dimensional world, be in one place at one instant, and at the next instant be in a different place, without having in some way passed over all of the space between.

In the same way, in regard to spiritual development, the older religions taught a way to be followed, a path to be traversed, toward the ultimate goal of "release," which corresponded in a sense to the Christian idea of "salvation" (before that idea was distorted by generations of priestly misinterpretation). They taught that all men who followed that way would reach the goal eventually, and that for those who were willing to make special efforts it would be possible to hasten the achievement, and reach the goal in a shorter time than the average. It is only among so-called Christian communities that we have the peculiar notion that there is some short cut to salvation, by which those people who have not yet developed themselves spiritually can be miraculously made fit for an eternity in purely spiritual realms.

Possibly the reason why this notion developed and gained such a strong foothold was that the Christian religion had somehow lost the old belief, shared by nearly all the ancient religions, in a long succession of earth lives, which would give a man sufficient time in which to develop the qualities needed for life in a spiritual "heaven." Believing that one life was all, and realizing how very few people reach a very high degree of spiritual development in their life on our present-day earth, its adherents had to figure out some scheme by which it would be possible to "save" some proportion of the unworthy ones. In the older religions, however, it was assumed that a man who was not yet ready for a purely spiritual life, when the time came for him to die, would return later for another life on this earth, and learn a little more, and return again and again until eventually the necessary point was reached.

In a later chapter, we will take up the discussion of this idea of reincarnation, or rebirth in a succession of physical bodies on this earth, and see how it fits in with the idea of progressive development or evolution, and why the concept of evolution is really imperfect and incomplete unless it includes this idea.

CHAPTER VI

THE BASIC IDEA OF PERIODICITY OR CYCLES

From consideration of the law of progressive development or evolution, we are led naturally to the related law of periodicity or cycles. H. P. Blavatsky (in *The Secret Doctrine*) phrased it thus: "This second assertion of the Secret Doctrine is the absolute universality of that law of periodicity, of flux and reflux, ebb and flow, which physical science has observed and recorded in all departments of nature. An alternation such as that of Day and Night, Life and Death, Sleeping and Waking, is a fact so common, so perfectly universal and without exception, that it is easy to comprehend that in it we see one of the absolutely fundamental laws of the Universe."

In our own bodies, we have the alternation of breathing in and out again, the systole and diastole of the heartbeat, and many less obvious rhythms. Even when we use our eyes, we alternately see and cease to see, although the period of change is so rapid as to give the illusion of continuity, but it is this periodical lapse of vision which makes it possible for motion pictures to seem continuous, by having the successive frames thrown on the screen at a rate which corresponds to the natural rhythm of our vision.

The earth turns on its axis, and at the same time travels around the sun, so that on successive days it is no longer in the same place. When the year is completed, and it returns to the same position, relative to the sun, astronomy tells us that it is only relatively the same, because in the meantime the sun itself has travelled a great distance. When we seek to understand the direction in which the sun travels, we find that it is part of a great galaxy, whose edges are marked to our vision by the Milky Way, and the galaxy as a whole seems to be shaped like a flattened-out disk, and to be spinning around its center. Besides its rotation, the galaxy as a whole also appears to have motion in relation to other galaxies. There seems to be no end to the complexities of movement. One thing we should note, however, is that while things seem to move in cycles or circles, actually the circles are always spirals, or helices, and things never come back quite to the same point where they started.

Applying this to the idea of the spiritual evolution of the universe, we find the occult statements – given fairly completely in the ancient Sanskrit writings, and only expressed in different words by modern writers – that there is an alternation of manifestation and withdrawal from manifestation. Figuratively speaking, these periods are sometimes called the "days and nights of Brahma." The period of "day," or manifestation, is described by the Sanskrit word *manvantara,* and the interval of "night" or rest in between is called *pralaya.* Furthermore, in the occult teaching it is understood that each *manvantara* takes up evolution where the preceding one ceased, and progress is carried forward in the successive cycles.

The traditional Hindu cosmogony worked out a very elaborate system, according to which a number of *manvantaras* make up a *maha-manvantara,* or great *manvantara,* and the corresponding number of *pralayas* are summed up, at the end of the great *manvantara,* by a *maha-,* or great *pralaya.* The ultimate beginning and end are beyond the power of thought – as far as thought can carry us, we see this periodicity, combined with the idea of gradual development and progress. Within each *manvantara* there are said to be cycles of alternating activity and rest for the solar systems, and for the globes in the solar systems, and for the life on those globes.

As for our own globe, we are told, in some books dealing with occult ideas on cosmogony, that its existence in manifestation falls into seven subdivisions or "rounds," and that at the present time we are somewhat past the middle of the fourth "round," which is supposedly the only one in which the globe of the earth has a dense physical form. In each round there are supposedly developed, in succession, seven great "human" types, each of which is called a "root race," and each root race is again supposed to be subdivided into seven subraces, which develop one after the other, with some overlapping.

There is supposed to have been a kind of "humanity," even in these first early (non-physical) rounds of our globe. This was naturally not in the form we ordinarily think of as human, but in sexless forms made up of subtle or non-physical "matter," in which the life essence which would ultimately be human (sometimes referred to as a "life wave") was gradually learning to inhabit (and acquire the power of control over) successively denser stages of matter. In the fourth or present round, it is said, the conditions of the earlier rounds were to a certain extent recapitulated in the first two root race periods, and those who were to be "men" possessed forms of astral or etheric rather than dense matter. Only in the middle of the so-called third root race did "men," inhabiting physical bodies, actually come into existence. There was some kind of merging of the mental aspects, which had developed in subtle bodies, with forms which had evolved physically, in the animal kingdom. There is supposed to have been involved in this process, in addition, some kind of transmission of "fire," or spiritual stimulation, from more highly evolved beings, the products of previous cycles of evolution. The story as transmitted by Madame Blavatsky appears to have been highly symbolical, and is made more confusing by the use of a great deal of "esoteric" terminology and words taken from some supposedly very ancient esoteric language.

Some later theosophical writers have worked out the scheme in great detail, and often use such terms as "fourth root race" to refer to the Mongoloid peoples and "fifth root race" to refer to the Caucasoids. There is also reference, in some books, to the future "sixth root race" which will follow our present type of humanity. Certain characteristics are supposed to be dominant in the nature of each of these subdivisions, and the sixth will supposedly show more intuitional ability than our present humanity, in which the practical mind is dominant. Precursors or forerunners of this future type are supposed to be coming into incarnation more and more as time passes. Interesting as some of these ideas may be, they can be found in other writings, and they are mentioned here only because they are sometimes referred to without explanation. Such details (like the details given in other chapters) are not regarded by the writer as actually part of the "basic ideas," but are included here to help in the interpretation or correlation of terminology found elsewhere.

There is one detail, however, in the statements given by H. P. Blavatsky, which is interesting, although it may be a mere coincidence. She states repeatedly and definitely that the beginning of the first physical race of humanity dates back to eighteen million years ago. Now, at the date she wrote (she died in 1891), scientific estimates of the length of the various geological epochs and periods were very different from today's estimates (eighteen million years ago was supposed to be around the beginning of the Jurassic, the age of the great dinosaurs). But it happens to be a fact that, by modern reckoning, the date of eighteen million years ago (now placed in the Miocene) would fit quite well as an approximate date for the separation of the zoological family of the Hominidae from the Pongidae, or the ancestral line leading to man from that leading to the modern great apes. The writer, therefore, has amused herself by speculating as to whether, if there were any original occult teaching on the subject, the account of the supposed beginning of humanity on earth, on "Lemuria," might not have actually referred to the earliest hominids. Examination of various fossil specimens indicates that populations which can be placed in the Hominidae (though not human in the modern sense) occurred at least some fifteen million years ago, both in East Africa (in Kenya) and in India (in the Siwalik deposits in the foothills of the Himalayas), and thus presumably in any intervening land areas also. On this basis, perhaps the following so-called "root race" might have been the various population groups of the species *Homo erectus* (formerly known as *Pithecanthropus),* and the present one might be, quite simply, *Homo sapiens.* This is, of course, a purely individual play of the imagination.

After this digression, we turn now to consideration of that aspect of the law of periodicity or cycles which is of most interest to us, because it is related to the life of individual men, and their gradual, progressive development of higher consciousness, or growth in awareness. Occultism teaches periodicity in all things. The universe has its *manvantara* and *pralaya,* and each solar system is said to have corresponding periods of development and activity, followed by rest and withdrawal. In human beings, among other rhythms, we find a daily alternation of waking and sleeping. But what of that other pair of opposites which is so important to every human being – life and death?

Westerners, who have for so long lost touch with the ancient teachings, commonly believe that there is only one life, followed by death which may mean annihilation or may mean "eternal life," in some heaven above the earth. (But where is "above" in relation to a globe spiraling in space?) Some still believe in the danger of eternal torment in "hell." But when we find periodicity, cycles of activity followed by rest, rhythmic alternation, everywhere else in the universe, why should human life be the one exception? Is life, perhaps, only a greater "day," and death only a longer "night" of rest and inner growth, to be followed by other "days" and "nights" in the long life of the soul?

That this is the true interpretation of life and death is a basic occult idea – an interesting hypothesis for those to whom the idea is new and strange, but often a relatively firm conviction for those who investigate deeply.

CHAPTER VII

THE BASIC IDEA OF REINCARNATION

Some Western people who have been brought up under the influence of orthodox religion have never heard of the theory of reincarnation, and others have heard of it only as some wild idea, held by the ignorant "heathen," that men's souls may be born again in the bodies of animals. Let it be stated at once that this latter concept is entirely contrary to the hypothesis which is believed by every true student of occultism to be no mere theory, but one of the basic laws of human existence.

As stated in the previous chapters, the theory of reincarnation, or repeated rebirths of the human spirit into embodied life on this earth, is wholly in harmony with, and analogous to, the concepts of biological evolution and the law of cycles. Indeed, without it these concepts seem, to the writer, to remain imperfect and incomplete.

The materialistic idea is that the concept of life apart from its material basis, in the matter perceptible to our physical senses, is only an illusion. But we have already demonstrated that this idea is untenable even scientifically, since it is matter itself which is the "illusion." Thus we come to the realization that the life which is expressed in any given form is just as "real" as the form itself. In fact, we see that in a very important sense the life is more real, because it seems to retain a fundamental identity throughout many changes of the form. Tom Jones at the age of sixty, since living cells continually renew themselves, uses a body which does not have in it the same material which was in the body of Tom Jones at thirty or forty, and which is an entirely different size and shape from the body of Tom Jones at the age of ten — or two. Yet no one, least of all Tom Jones himself, would doubt that it was the same "individual" functioning all the time. It is not the continuity of shape or material which gives the continuity of the life. The life uses the physical body as a musician uses his instrument – as a vehicle for self-expression. When the instrument is no longer adequate – when its utilization is rendered impossible by defects in operation caused by accident or disease – then the life departs, and the body "dies." But the life remains capable of taking up a new instrument.

If matter as we know it – the physical matter studied by physical science – is not the only kind of substance in the universe, but merely the densest kind, then we have no valid reason to deny the possibility of a continuity of conscious life after the death of the physical body. The inner spirit can be conceived of as functioning, and expressing itself, in vehicles formed of the matter of the subtle "planes." The question then is whether the human spirit, which has lived for perhaps seventy years in a dense physical body, will continue to live after "death" in subtle or spiritual realms for an endless eternity, or whether at some future time it will take another physical body for further experience on our "lower earth."

We may look into the beliefs of the ancient religions and the beliefs of the mystics, and into the writings of many of the great thinkers and poets of the modern world, and we shall find that the second idea is dominant in the former, and quite common in the latter. But let us consider the idea itself, and its innate reasonableness.

In the first place, if it is possible for a human spirit to live adequately and happily in an eternal "heaven," after one short life on earth, what was the point or use in having the earth life at all? Earthly life is full of difficulties and troubles, and in comparison with the possibility of an eternity of bliss, it would seem to be something in the nature of a mistake on the part of the creator, who might just as easily have created angelic creatures who would live always in higher regions, and never have to undergo the nuisance and pain of human life. But religion (among civilized men) postulates a Creator who is wise and loving, not one who would subject his creatures to pain and stress for no reason, just as an idle experiment or bit of cruel sport. There must be some reason, in the divine plan, to explain why the human spirit, which is one in its inner being with the Great Self of the universe—a spark of the One Flame—should incarnate in the very first place. Why should a spark of the divine encase itself in a dense and clumsy form, and go through the experience of all sorts of limitations and difficulties?

Using the great law of analogy, let us realize that power is built up, and increases, by increase of resistance. Steam which is allowed to escape freely into the atmosphere never accomplishes anything. If we want to have steam power, we must confine the steam within limitations, and build up the pressure against those limitations, and then release it only in the direction in which we wish to release it, under firm control. If an athlete wishes to develop strong muscles, he practices using his muscles against something which resists his efforts, and thus his strength grows. It is useless to multiply examples, as the general principle should be perfectly clear. Applying this now to the idea of spiritual strength, we can see that the difficulties and limitations of earthly life are not really an obstacle to the development of the life of the spirit within the form, but constitute in reality the very thing which makes such development possible. In a region of eternal bliss, spirit would remain diffuse and nebulous—it is only the resistance of matter which enables the spirit to develop that definiteness and strength which makes possible the existence of individual souls rather than merely some vague general all-soul.

If we understand this, we see why the human spirit incarnates, and takes to itself a body of physical substance. It seeks to acquire from life on earth the benefits which only such a life can bestow. But now we begin to observe the inconsistencies and apparent injustices of life, as it appears superficially. One person lives an interesting, varied life, full of all sorts of experiences, and dies at an advanced age, having presumably learned a great deal. Another dies at

birth, or soon thereafter. Still another may live for a reasonably long period of time, but with a life so fixed in rou-
tine and so uneventful that he is hardly more alive than a
domesticated animal. Another may be born in a slum environment, from degenerate parents, and grow up almost
inevitably into a criminal. He has experiences of a sort, to
be sure, but it is hardly the type of experience to fit his soul
for eternal life in the realms of spirit.

The utter absurdity and senselessness of a procedure
which would find one earth life, and only one, necessary for
spiritual development, and yet give different people such
entirely different samplings of earth life, seems so obvious
that it is hard to understand how the Christian church ever
managed to retain its hold upon the Western mind for so
many centuries, without any more sensible explanation of
the purpose of life. Truly, the so-called religious teachers
of the West (apart from some unorthodox individuals in
recent decades) have been merely blind leaders of the blind.
All the time, the logical and reasonable explanation remained part of the great religions of the East, even though
there too the influence of priestcraft and ignorance and
superstition inevitably brought about foolishness in details.

Life is a school for souls. But a child does not go to school
for only one day, and then think that his school life is ended,
and that he can now proceed to go on with life in the adult
world! Not even does he go to school for only one term, but
he returns again and again, each time learning new lessons,
and being promoted from one grade to the next as he grows
older, if he works at the normal rate. Not all children are in
the same grade, but they are not all the same age either.

If some mythical being from another universe could
look down on earth through a super-telescope and focus on
the life in a school for just one day, he would observe many
apparent injustices and inequalities. Some children might
be drilling over and over on simple and uninteresting elementary facts, such as the multiplication tables. Others
might be doing experiments in science, in the higher grades,
or working at art or music or dramatics. Some would be

struggling hard to learn things which were so well known to others as to be taken for granted. Our mythical observer might well say: "Every one should have an equal chance. This system is not fair at all." But we could answer: "My dear sir, you merely fail to take a long enough view of the matter. What you see is only one day. These children who are now in the higher grades, for whom so many things seem easy, are merely older. They have attended the school for a longer time, and in the past they too had the same simple lessons as those at which you now see the little ones working. These little ones in their turn will go ahead from one grade to the next, and some day they too will stand at the top, with the entire course duly completed."

Do you see the analogy to human life? In life we see some individuals who are very undeveloped and simple, who seem to take a long time to learn even the simplest things. We see other people who are gifted with high intelligence and all sorts of innate talents, who learn swiftly and easily. Life is a school for souls. The first individuals mentioned are the little ones – the younger souls; the others are the older souls who have already attended the school for many sessions, and mastered the simple lessons, and who are now doing advanced work. But the young souls will grow older, and their turn will come. If we find different human beings at different levels of development – in different "grades" – it is because of a difference in the age of their souls, and sometimes a little because some have worked more eagerly and earnestly than their fellows who are content just to "get by," just as in school we find a few children who are in a higher grade than is normal for their age. When we see only one earth life, we are failing to take a long enough view, just like our mythical observer with the super-telescope. If "a thousand years are as but a day" in the sight of God, so also one life on earth is but a day in the long life of a human soul.

The law of periodicity is applicable here, in that each "day" is followed by a "night" of rest and enjoyment at home – for the higher regions are the true home of the soul, and earth only the place of its schooling. There is never an eternity of night and rest, but an alternation from one phase to the other at periodic intervals, and whenever morning comes again there is a renewal of outer activity.

With reference to the other basic concept of progressive development, or evolution, is it not inconsistent to deny the "special creation" of animal species, and then believe in the possibility of a special creation of individual souls, one for each new human being born, through all the ages of human life? Physically and biologically, we know that complicated structures are always built up slowly and gradually from less complicated ones. Consider then the enormous complexity of the mental life of a well-developed, civilized man. Leaving aside for the moment the question of spirit, or "soul life," and thinking only of the intellect, does it not seem incredible that one could start from nothing, at the moment of conception or birth (whichever you prefer to take), and in the space of twenty or thirty years develop that complex structure which is a civilized mind? And then think of those cases which are beyond the average—the genius who may be further removed from the mental level of a savage, in some ways, than the savage is from that of an ape. Think of the fact that in the case of genius we sometimes find, in the mind of a mere child of four or five, complex powers of consciousness surpassing those of many adults. How could the mind grow from absolute nothingness to that level in a few short years? The concept that consciousness also is a product of gradual evolutionary growth seems almost to be forced upon us.

The explanation given by students of occultism is that there is indeed an evolution of consciousness and inner life, just as surely as there is an evolution of form. The life uses a form adapted to its needs, and discards it when it is outgrown, and then returns a little later in a form which is a little better. When the Divine Spirit "involves" itself in matter, cycling into denser and denser form, there is at first no differentiation into individual souls. The life essence gradually differentiates into different types or groups, and these in turn divide into a larger number of smaller groups, just as the sap of a tree flows up the one main trunk, and then into a number of branches, and thence into the subdivisions of the smaller branches. The "soul" of a plant or animal is a part of a "group soul," and when the individual plant or animal dies, and the life essence departs from the form, that life essence returns to and is merged in the "group soul" of that particular species or variety. Whatever lessons the particular life may have taught – say for instance the lesson that a hawk can kill a baby chicken – will be somehow incorporated into the "collective unconscious" of the group, and the accumulation of many similar experiences in different individual forms will result in the formation of a specific "animal instinct." Every new form born into that species (or "population group" within a species) will bear within itself an "unconscious" racial memory of all the previous forms of the group.

It is only when we reach the human level that we have "individualization." Each human soul now in existence (either in physical life or in life in the subtle worlds) was "individualized" at some period in the remote past, the dates differing in different cases, so that some souls are comparatively young, and some older, and some few a great deal older. The process according to which this individualization took place has been described in great detail in certain modern books dealing with occultism, but it seems to the writer that such unverifiable statements need not be taken seriously. The writers are using words for something outside of normal human experience, and all our words were built up to indicate shared ordinary experience, and can never truly describe any experience which transcends the ordinary. Also, modern statements have probably been reported through a long sequence of teachers, with the possibility of error due to imperfect transmission at each step.

In any case, the details are irrelevant, for all except advanced students. The thing we need to grasp is the main simple idea. This is that at some point in the development of animal-man a stage is reached when the inner life which has been in some separate body breaks away (or buds off) from that of the group of which it has previously formed a part, and one particular "spark" of the Divine Spirit is somehow attracted by this separation to enter into it and impregnate it with its own divine qualities – not in complete expression, of course, but potentially. Thereafter the former animal-man is truly a human being, with an individual human soul.

Perhaps actually, for hundreds of thousands of years after "animal-men" or proto-humans had become human in the sense of being able to make crude chipped stone tools, their consciousness was still not truly individualized, and the tribal or group "soul" still merged the experiences of its members, while true "individualization" came at a later date, in isolated cases, when some member of the tribe met with a really distinct experience sufficiently crucial to cause a real mental "budding off." We probably can never be sure of such details. The essential point is that the date of individualization is thought to have been quite different in different cases.

The speed of each man's spiritual evolution, after individualization, may also vary, according to circumstances, and according to the degree of effort which he exerts in the attempt to "realize" the potential divinity within him. However, it is never possible for a human soul to return to life in an animal form. That is a misconception.

The belief in reincarnation is held, in some form or other, by the majority of the human race. Many religions which preceded Christianity included this belief as a basic ingredient in their system of thought. It is held by some quite primitive people, in a primitive way, and on the other hand it was set forth with considerable sophistication in the ancient religion of India – the Hinduism of the Vedas and the Upanishads. The teachings of the Buddha, since their emphasis was upon methods of psychological development, did not deal particularly with reincarnation because the idea was completely taken for granted.

The Buddha taught "the Way" to obtain "release" from

the necessity of rebirth, which obviously took for granted that rebirth was the normal occurrence. Some contemporary Buddhist sects, of the Southern or Theravada group, teach that there is no soul, but merely "qualities" which reincarnate into a new body immediately upon the death of the old one, but scholars have shown that this is contrary to the original teachings. The Buddha himself seems to have held personal ideas very much like those of the Upanishads, but to have been intent upon practical ethical ends in his instructions to his followers. In the translation of the original Buddhist scriptures into Pali, with the Pali version becoming the basis for the Buddhism of such countries as Ceylon, Burma, and Thailand, the distinction between the higher Self of man, which is one with the Universal Self, and the lower personal self which depends upon the conditions of one particular earth life, somehow became lost or obscured. Statements made in the original teachings about the "unreality" and impermanence of the lower self became reinterpreted to lead to the conclusion that there is no "soul" and no "life after death." Proponents of this view seem to overlook its lack of logic, because if there is no real Self, there is nothing which needs to be "liberated." Reincarnation is basic to true Buddhism.

Belief in reincarnation was also an intrinsic part of the systems of Pythagoras and various other Greek philosophers, and was regularly taught in all the mystery schools of the ancient religions, including those of early Christianity. It was not until some five centuries after the origin of Christianity, when it had long been the state religion of Rome, that the belief in reincarnation was formally declared to be not according to orthodox dogma.

A detailed discussion of all of this past history of religions can be found in Blavatsky's *Isis Unveiled* and *The Secret Doctrine*, where one may find her explanation of why the belief was thrown out of the Christian Church. The loss of this belief accounts for much of the degradation of the Dark Ages in Europe, and, indirectly, for the destructive materialism of the present day, which results to a great extent from a rational intellectual revolt against the unjust and irrational system which was all that was left in orthodox Christianity.

Many of the greatest thinkers and poets of Europe and America have refound this belief for themselves, and traces of it appear in their works in many places. But the lack of a complete and systematic exoteric teaching anywhere in the West, in the past, has made their formulation of it dependent upon their own individual intuition. At the present time, we are fortunate in that much of the old Inner Wisdom has, during the past century, actually been brought to light and made accessible in books. Thus, we may hope eventually to have a clearer and better organized presentation. However, the most important books are difficult to study, and the older ones usually contain much extraneous or out-of-date material. Probably as a result of this, much of the present-day writing upon the subject of reincarnation seems to have been done by people who have made little or no study of the available material, and often seem to be completely ignorant of it. Thus, the statements found in many contemporary books reflect only their authors' personal ideas, which may be quite confused and distorted—based solely on experiments in hypnotic regression, for example, or solely upon statements made by some one in trance. Thus, what these books present as the theory of reincarnation is often an utter travesty.

The belief in reincarnation which is held by occultists is the belief that an individual human soul passes through a great number (many hundreds or thousands) of successive incarnations as a human being, with alternating periods in the subtle worlds, gradually developing from savagery through barbarism to civilization, and finally flowering in the perfected man who has nothing more to learn from life on earth, but is "graduated" from the school of human life, having fitted himself to enter a kingdom beyond that of the human kingdom. The individual soul is not specially "created," but derives from the group soul by a natural process of "budding off," and the group soul in its turn was derived from some more comprehensive group soul which is a manifestation of the All-Soul. The individual soul is not separately "immortal," in the Christian sense, because some day, in the far future, each of the individualized selves will overcome what the Buddhists call "the delusion of separateness" and shed the garment or chrysalis which separates it from awareness of its unity with others and with the Divine Self, and separated individuality for that self will no longer exist as such. The human spirit is immortal—being essentially one with the Universal Spirit—but it is not bounded or separated. The exact relationships between spirit, soul, and body are so truly "occult" as to be incomprehensible to the ordinary mind, but it is the conviction of all students of true occultism that Nirvana, or the "blowing out" of separated individuality, will not mean cessation, or any loss at all, but only a greater expansion of consciousness.

CHAPTER VIII

THE BASIC IDEA OF JUSTICE

One of the most potent arguments for belief in the theory of reincarnation is the demonstration of its complete harmony with man's innate desire for justice.

If all souls were created, originally, each at the beginning of the life of one human being on earth, and their ultimate fate, for all eternity, depended upon the use they made of that one earthly life, what a monstrous and cruel farce the world would be! For some men are born under conditions which exclude them from all possibility of high spiritual development, whereas others are born under conditions which give them every advantage. Some are victims of malnutrition (or their mothers' use of drugs) even before birth, and are never capable of normal mental development, while others are born well nourished and physically perfect, and given the care which enables them to reach an optimum development. Some live to a ripe old age, others die in youth, or even as tiny infants. With all of these differences, would it be fair for any higher power to judge all men alike at the close of this one life, and decide, merely upon the basis of the results achieved, what their fate shall be for all eternity?

In the innermost nature of any human being who has not been "conditioned" out of it, there is a strong fundamental demand that the universe should make sense, and that justice should prevail. The idea that "God moves in a mysterious way," and that therefore people should be humble and meek, and submit uncomplainingly to all sorts of troubles and indignities without investigating their cause or trying to correct them, because such is "the will of God," is, in the opinion of the writer, so pernicious an idea that its espousal by the Christian Church is one of the most harmful aspects of Christianity—one which has done untold and immeasurable damage to human development. People need to be whole and integrated, active and self-reliant, willing to take chances and to accept the consequences if they have made a mistake, with a forward-looking eagerness based upon complete and assured confidence that they will get desirable results if their actions are "right."

It is a law of nature, at the biological level, that unpleasantness is associated with wrong actions, actions which would lead to harm to the individual or to the species, but that actions which "permit or promote further development," and which contribute to survival and growth, are felt as pleasant. This is one of the beautiful results of natural selection. Whenever an individual animal happened to be attracted to something actually bad for it, it would not survive as well, or be as likely to produce offspring, as a competitor attracted only by something which contributed to survival and growth. Through the course of the ages, the effects of such selection accumulated, in each evolutionary line. Therefore each species now living has an inherent tendency to be attracted towards, and to feel as "pleasant," objects or activities which are actually good for it, and to reject those which might do it harm.

Every one instinctively recognizes that this should apply at the human level also, and that really "right" actions should bring happiness. But human life and relationships are so complex that the results of an action are not always closely associated with it in time. The same rule holds for humanity as for all the other species on earth, but for human individuals the results of action are sometimes delayed for so long that the connection is not easy to see. Therefore, we human beings are in urgent need of a philosophical belief which will give us faith that the law still holds. We need a strong conviction that "wrong" actions cannot possibly be good for us in the long run, but that if we persist in doing "right," that is, in doing things which permit or promote development instead of frustrating it (for ourselves or others, since others are part of our own larger self, speaking sociologically as well as from the occult standpoint), the pleasant results will surely come. This conviction becomes easier to reach through the concepts of reincarnation and karma.

In physical science, we are familiar with the rule that for every action there is an equal and opposite reaction. We usually think of this law only in connection with physical force. But the occult position is that the law holds good just as inexorably for action, or force, exerted upon emotional or mental levels. In writing upon occult subjects, this law is usually referred to as the law of karma. *Karma* is an old Sanskrit word, literally meaning "action" or "work," but the word includes in itself this idea that action always implies, or is balanced by, a corresponding reaction. This Sanskrit word seems to fit the occult concept better than any English word, because it has been used, in the occult sense, in India, for thousands of years. It is therefore adopted into modern English by occult writers, and the adjective "karmic" formed from it to mean "pertaining to karma." For those who do not yet know all the connotations of the Sanskrit word, "justice" may convey the essential idea more clearly, and therefore this term has been used in the beginning here.

Christianity stresses the concept of the "forgiveness of sins," but it seems to the writer that for any "right-minded" person, it would be much more satisfactory to feel sure of justice! It is true that the Christian scriptures also teach that "Whatsoever a man sows, that shall he also reap," and this is indeed a statement of one of the great laws of the universe, although many people disregard it. Some refuse to believe it, and consider that the facts of life disprove it. However, even during the course of one life, it is often possible to trace the workings of this law, and to perceive that the circumstances which come to a man at one stage of his life have been caused, quite fully and precisely, by actions and decisions he made in the past. But sometimes a man sows causes for which there is no time to reap the results in the same life. In this case, the results appear in a later life, apparently without cause, but only apparently so.

If a man performs certain actions one day, and then goes home and goes to sleep, the results will appear the day afterward, or even many days later, and the fact that he has been asleep in the meantime does not break the relationship between cause and effect. Even so, the "sleep" which is called death, though it does usually break the connection of conscious memory, does not break the continuity of the individual existence as the same real individual, and the causes set going in one life bring about completely just results in a later life. Human life is too complex, and each human being has too many complicated relationships with too many other human beings, for one short life to enable all of these relationships to be worked out and perfectly balanced. Nevertheless, most of the results which a man reaps are caused by his own actions in the same life. And if a man sets himself to act rightly, he can be sure of good results fairly soon, without waiting for a future life.

It is however obvious that, although we can often perceive the workings of the law of cause and effect in particular circumstances, there are many things in life which do not seem to fit with any ultimate law of "justice," if we believe that each individual actually has "only one life to live." Indeed, for many rational individuals, the idea of a "just God" becomes a mockery and a farce. It is logically impossible to reconcile the idea of only one life on earth, and a subsequent eternal reward or punishment, with belief in divine justice and a universe of law, because people so obviously do not get an even start. The attempt to make such a reconciliation leads either to agnostic pessimism and cynicism, or to an unconscious schizophrenia which colors and distorts all other attempts at logical thinking. Only with the belief in reincarnation is it possible to reconcile the apparent inconsistencies of earthly life with a real belief in ultimate justice.

In his book *The Next Development in Man*, L. L. Whyte discusses what he calls the "European dissociation" and the need for a "unitary philosophy." Many writers in recent years have tried to formulate such a philosophy, and such attempts are valuable because they help to clear away past errors, but none of them is complete, or really adequate as a substitute for the crippling dogmas of religion. They offer no explanation of death, no assurance of a continuity of love relationships or of an ultimate justice which would make individual effort worthwhile. It seems to the writer that the occult philosophy offers the only adequate philosophy of life for the scientifically oriented, open-minded, spiritually sensitive young people of today who are the vanguard of the more advanced human race of tomorrow.

People who have grown up with the idea that there is only one earth life, which is followed either by annihilation or by some mysterious life in spiritual regions, have often ceased to expect justice in human life, in spite of the fact that the human spirit instinctively craves it. For such people, the idea that everything in the universe works by natural law, and that there is no such thing as "chance" (in the sense of something happening without cause), is so strange that it is a little hard to grasp. Therefore the occult concept of karma needs some explanation. There is also the problem of how this concept may be related to that other fundamental desire of the human spirit — the desire to feel that it is free to make its own destiny, and not a mere automaton.

Even in the minds of people who are familiar with the word, many misconceptions about the law of karma exist. For example, some people think that to believe in karma means to believe that the actions of past lives have set an inflexible pattern for this one, and therefore that nothing a man can do now will make any real difference in the results due to him. This is more or less the same as believing in "kismet" or fate, and may lead to hopelessness and lack of effort. But the correct concept is really quite different. Sometimes, also, a distorted idea about the action of karma may offer an excuse for not trying to help others, on the theory that these other people are merely getting their karmic deserts, and that no one has any duty, or even any right, to interfere,

Now it is just as impossible to "interfere" with the law of karma as with the law of gravitation. And it is just as possible to utilize a real understanding of the law, in order to achieve some desired result. Allowing for the fact that man's evolution is not yet completed, and therefore some things are as yet beyond his capacity, a man can make his own destiny, even in his present life. He most certainly makes his own ultimate destiny. Man does have free will, and the law of karma does not abrogate this free will in any sense. Certain actions bring certain results, according to the law, but it is the man himself who decides in the first place what action he will take!

If any man has hanging over him a weight of "bad karma" from past misdeeds, whether in this or previous incarnations, it is always possible to offset and "balance" this by deeds in the correct direction. He need not, and should not, sit idly by and wait for the results of the past to appear, because at every moment of his life, the future passes through that dividing line which we call the present, and itself becomes a part of the past, to be added to, and balanced up against, all the other previous parts of the past. Thus the past *can be modified,* by the future which will join it. It is man's task to guide and control his own future actions, in the light of increasing understanding. Every man can say, with perfect truth, "I am the master of my fate, I am the captain of my soul."

Karma is frequently spoken of as being good or bad, but in reality all karma is good, in the sense that it is the inevitable working of a law which maintains the balance of the universe. What people mean by the expression "good karma" is that pleasant results will come from "good" actions, while bad karma implies the unpleasant results to be expected from "bad" actions. However, even unpleasant results could be considered good karma, in one sense, because useful, when one has made a mistake, to indicate that fact, and to suggest the need for a change of direction or procedure.

Many books have been written upon the subject of karma, some in the form of essays, and some in the form of fiction, or stories which illustrate the working of the law. We can do little more than touch upon the subject here, its complexities are so vast.

One very crude illustration sometimes given is that a man who causes a violent death to another makes himself liable to meet with a violent death later. Some writers on the subject have said that if his action was really impersonal, as for example in battle, the results to him might come from an impersonal source, in a way which seemed to be a mere accident, but that if it was a deliberate, personal murder, it would be necessary for him to meet that same individual later on and adjust the account with that particular individual, because strong emotions form strong karmic ties. This does not necessarily mean, however, that he must be murdered in turn by the man he had murdered. There are various ways in which a past evil may be "balanced" by a corresponding good. For example, and again this is a very crude illustration, to save a man's life in one incarnation would atone for having caused him to lose it prematurely in some previous one. But the point is that many deaths which seem to be undeserved are explicable as the paying off of past karmic debts, incurred perhaps very long ago. All men in their early incarnations must have done a good deal of killing.

If a man is kind to his fellow creatures, in a physical way, that will supposedly contribute to making him deserve a life where he will be physically comfortable and well-to-do. On the other hand, difficult circumstances may sometimes be required in order to bring out the growth of certain capacities, whereas a life of ease might lack stimulus and therefore not contribute much towards progress. The whole subject is exceedingly complex, with many factors interweaving to produce the visible result. One other particular example, however, which is often mentioned, is that if a man works hard at the development of some particular capacity, in one life, he will be born thereafter with a natural "talent" in that line. This accounts for the genius, whose ability is no accident, but the well-deserved result of a long period of intensive effort.

The well-rounded, highly intelligent man is the product of a long series of lives, during which he has had many types of experience, and has learned the lessons which those experiences taught. Although sometimes an "old soul" may, in order to work out some particular karmic debt, be born with some special handicap, in general the people of low intelligence and comparatively undisciplined reactions are "young" as souls. This means that their individualization occurred more recently. They will require a larger number of future lives in order to reach the peak of merely human achievement, but since they started later, there is no injustice involved.

Thus, while the occultist believes that "all men are created equal" in one sense, in that each one bears within himself a spark of the divine life which is capable of being fanned into a flame, he considers that men are not at all equal at any given moment of time, but that different individuals stand upon different rungs of the ladder of evolution. All men are brothers, and should act toward each other as brothers in a loving family would act, but human souls are of different "ages." Belief in human brotherhood should not preclude the use of intelligent discrimination in adapting environmental pressures or opportunities to fit the different needs of different stages of growth. Naturally, the point at which any individual stands is an individual matter, and cannot be judged by skin color or membership in a particular cultural group. An "old soul," or highly advanced individual, might incarnate purposely in a relatively undeveloped group, in order to serve there. However, for those who feel themselves to be handicapped in some way, the prospect of many future opportunities should serve as a corrective for discouragement. Not everything has to be accomplished in this one life, because this life is not the only one, there will be plenty of others!

Some people identify themselves so strongly with their physical selves, and the personality connected with one life, that they find the occult concept offers little comfort. They say that if you cannot remember what you did in your previous lives, the results which come to you are still not just, and that if you are going to be a "different person" in a future life, it does not matter what results you may be sowing for yourself by your actions in this life. This question of memory will be discussed later. What the occultist considers to be the "real" self does remember, and the feeling of identification with the lower personality, or even with the actual physical body, which some people have, is one of the "delusions" which the occult teaching is designed to overcome.

The occultist's concept of his "self," or the "self" of any other individual, is not restricted to the personal self of one particular earth life. He thinks of the "real individual" as having his true home in the "upper mental" or *arupa* (Sanskrit for "formless") levels, and of the personality as simply a "projection" from a higher-dimensional reality. Or, to use a different metaphor, he thinks of his soul as an actor who has played many roles, who has some one role to play in this particular earth life, but who can readily lay aside the costume which he wore for this role and prepare to take a different one for a different role. The circumstances which affect the character in the play, or damage done to the costume for one play, will not harm his essential self, which has been in many such plays, and will be in many more.

The decisions made, and the actions taken, in any one earth life, are of real importance, because they contribute their weight to the whole of his karma, and may have an important effect upon how long it takes him to reach the "graduation" point, but they are not of that critical importance which they seem to have for people who believe that their fate for all eternity depends upon their attitudes in this life. No individual can ever act so mistakenly as to deprive himself completely of the opportunity for a future turn in the right direction. All men are the "sons of God," and "all His sons will one day reach His feet, however far they stray."

CHAPTER IX

THE BASIC IDEA OF LIFE IN THE SUBTLE WORLDS

Now we come to one of the most important questions in life—that question to which no philosophy except the occult teaching gives an adequate reply—the question of what happens after death. Science does not know, philosophers merely theorize, religions claim to know but can offer no real evidence. It is only the Inner Wisdom—which was formerly taught in the schools of religious "mysteries," which is held in its entirety only by those perfected men known as the Masters of the Wisdom, and which has been partially revealed to the modern world through Madame Blavatsky and other pupils of those Masters—which can give the answer we seek.

For the reader who is not yet convinced of the existence of such an Inner Wisdom, the following statements will have to be regarded merely as theories—though it is to be hoped that they will prove interesting theories. Deeper study of writings based on this Wisdom may gradually lead to intellectual belief, but real conviction and confirmation must wait for that development of the spiritual intuition which brings the student eventually to the sure guidance of those who *know*.

The writers of the ancient scriptures of the world were all Knowers, in various degrees, but each wrote for the people of a particular time and place, and modern translators, lacking that general grasp of the subject which would give them the clue to the real meaning of the words used, have not been able, as a rule, to translate any such scriptures into a form which gives a clear understanding to the modern reader. The ancient scriptures of India approach it most closely, because a great deal of the occult tradition has been handed down through the ages by generations of Sanskrit scholars, along with the actual scriptures themselves. But the modern world is chiefly indebted to H. P. Blavatsky, and to those who gave her her mission, for a presentation of the subject in a new and more complete form.

According to the teaching thus given forth, every human being has seven "principles," and the dense body is merely a sort of outer overcoat utilized by the spirit to incarnate in the physical world, in order to function in it and learn the lessons which could be learned only through the experience of earthly life. But when "death" ensues, the man himself remains essentially the same – he has merely discarded his overcoat.

As mentioned in Chapter IV, we are told that in and through the dense body, during life, there is something called the "etheric body" or "vital body," which is not really a body at all, but a sort of shining network of vital force, which is the real carrier of physical vitality and sensation. The Sanskrit word *prana* is taken over by some writers as a name for the force itself. At death this complex of energy gathers itself together and withdraws from the dense body, passing out through the crown of the head, and is finally severed from it. At the same time, all of the more subtle material – matter of the astral, mental, and higher planes – which during life had interpenetrated the material making up the physical body – likewise withdraws. The consciousness or inner life remains sheathed in this more subtle matter, since the network of vitality pertains really to the physical plane, and gradually disintegrates after its withdrawal from the physical body. (It has been suggested that the not-yet-scattered shape of the "etheric body" may be the vague shape of light sometimes reported as having been seen near a grave.)

Ordinarily, there is a period of unconsciousness, during the time that this withdrawal of the subtle bodies is taking place. When the man regains consciousness, perhaps after only a few minutes or perhaps after several hours (or even days if the death was sudden and violent), he finds himself sensitive to the vibrations of the plane next finer than the physical plane—that plane which is spoken of as the "emotional plane" or "astral world," and which in Sanskrit is called *kamaloka,* meaning "the place of desire." The reason he is thus sensitive to impressions from this emotional world is that his strongest and densest sheath is now that one which is made up of "matter" which pertains to that world. He always had such a sheath of astral matter when he was alive, but unless he was what is called psychic he was unconscious of its vibrations, because the vibrations received by his five senses from physical matter were so much heavier as to drown them out. Now, however, he has discarded his physical body, and impressions from the astral world begin to pour in upon him.

We are familiar with the fact that in the field of sound we have a phenomenon called "sympathetic vibration." If you cause a direct vibration of one musical string, another which is nearby, if it is tuned to the same pitch, will start to vibrate without any contact except that of the sound waves. It is by a similar effect of sympathetic vibration that impressions are conveyed in the astral world, and reach the inner consciousness of the real man. In the sheath of astral matter which is now his vehicle, he will have astral material of different degrees of fineness, capable of vibrating at different rates. Each type will be responsive to and will react to a certain type of vibration from the astral "atmosphere," and his consciousness will receive the corresponding impressions.

In the astral plane, as in all the other great planes of the cosmos, there are said to be seven subdivisions or so-called subplanes. Each of these subplanes of the astral plane is made up of matter which is stimulated and thrown into motion by a different type (or "level") of emotion. Symbolically speaking, the astral world was referred to in old writings as "water," because its material is fluidic—constantly moving and changing. We are told that every emotion sends out waves or ripples of a characteristic color. These spread out in all directions at once, forming a sort of succession of expanding spheres of colored light, which gradually weaken and disappear when struck by cross-currents from other centers. Apart from this continual crossing and intermingling of emotional waves from different centers, every emotion which is connected with a definite thought is said to create also, in the matter of the astral world (and in that of the mental world at the same time), a shape called a "thought form." These may be simple or "abstract" geometric shapes, which may have a symbolical significance, or they may be images, in astral matter, of various persons or objects. Some thought forms tend to float around near their creator, if they have not been particularly "directed" anywhere, but others travel toward the person or object toward which the thought was directed. The nature of the thought form depends upon the nature of the emotion or thought which called it into being, and its vividness and the amount of time it retains its definite shape depend upon the intensity of the emotion connected with it. Continuous renewal of the emotion or thought, in identical form, could serve to maintain a "thought form" in apparent "life" for a lengthy period. We are told that some "thought forms" which have been reinforced by the combined thoughts and emotions of many people — the apparent personality of Hamlet or Robin Hood for example — might seem to exist upon the astral plane as vividly as the form of any actual or "real" person. For this reason also, the astral world is particularly called the world of *maya* or illusion, its forms being more illusory even than those of physical matter.

In the case of a man newly dead, unless he is sufficiently advanced to have some conscious control over the organization of his astral sheath, there is no sensitivity to all levels of the astral world at once, but only to a fragment of it. Some writers explain this by saying that the material of this sheath tends to arrange itself (after physical death) in concentric layers or shells, with the densest and heaviest matter on the outside, and thus a man who has a great deal of "lower" emotion will be encased and limited at first by astral matter which responds only to the sights and sounds (or what seem to him sights and sounds) of the lowest astral subplane. This experience corresponds to the religious idea of purgatory, and in extreme cases even to the idea of hell, except that it is temporary. A murderer might seem to see his victim pursuing him in his turn, a chronic drunkard might tend to see frightening or monstrous forms similar to those seen in drunken delirium, while victims of other low vices would receive sensations corresponding to their particular vice.

This unhappy after-death experience is not a punishment inflicted by some arbitrary power, but simply a psychological "projection" of "thought forms" from the man himself, resulting from the fact that during life he built into himself the material of such low or degrading emotions. However, even in the worst cases, this material is never all that he has. There is usually some emotion of love or tenderness for some one, and that too receives its inevitable result, in time, because the lower or "heavier" particles are gradually thrown off—evaporated, in a sense—into the general material of the plane, and then the man's outer sheath is composed of material of the better type, and he awakens to sights and sounds of a more pleasant nature. In the case of an ordinary fairly good man, the amount of this lower or coarser material is not enough, even in the beginning, to transmit complete impressions from the lowest level and block out the finer vibrations, and therefore he will awaken to consciousness, after his passage through death, in that level of the astral world which contains thought structures and forms corresponding more or less to the physical world. Some writers claim that he may not at first even realize that he is dead, until gradually he begins to notice inconsistencies and become sensitive to things which he knows could not be physical. As time passes, he too gradually loses the material which was the lowest for him, and gradually awakens more and more to the higher astral levels, where there is no longer any representation of earthly scenes and structures, but where there are representations of the ideas constructed by different religions about "paradise." People who have been of a scientific rather than religious turn of mind may be surrounded by "wish fulfillment" thought forms connected with their own interests.

The astral world is said to be inhabited not only by "dead" people, but by the astral sheaths of living people (and animals) also. A dead man cannot see physical bodies, but can see the similar-looking astral forms of living people. (Although the shape of the "aura" is said to be ovoid, its outer part is composed of only a small amount of the astral material, most of which is gathered into a form duplicating that of the physical body which it penetrates.) These astral bodies, visible to the dead man, will be deaf and blind to astral impressions while the people are awake, but may be utilized as a focus of consciousness when they are asleep. (In sleep only the "etheric body" remains in the dense one, the others withdraw.) This is true, at least, of people who are comparatively well developed. Those who are not are said to have sheaths which tend to stay near the sleeping bodies, brooding within themselves and not really awake to any impressions from the surrounding astral environment. But the consciousness of an advanced man, when the finer sheaths have withdrawn themselves from his sleeping body, may be sufficiently "awake" on the astral plane for a dead person to communicate with him. He may or may not remember this as a "dream." (In most cases, however, dreams which are remembered do not bring through impressions from any astral or higher level experience, but are merely confused, although sometimes symbolical, rearrangements made by the brain of memories or impressions which originally came from some physical source.) He may remember nothing about other experiences in the astral world until he himself dies (because of the difficulty of "bringing through" to the physical brain impressions made on the higher sheaths), but at death he will "awaken" to a world which he will recognize as not really strange at all, but merely the world in which, as he will now remember, he has been "living" during his sleep every night! It must be remembered that the astral world is not in a different "place," but interpenetrates the physical world, so that astral beings are really around us all the time. Since the astral world extends farther than the physical globe, however, some parts of it actually are "above" us.

In addition to human beings, the astral world is said to have its own inhabitants, that is, a host of beings at different levels of spiritual evolution which are not human, and which have no dense bodies, but which are nevertheless an important part of nature, on another line of evolution. These beings are called variously "elementals" or nature spirits of different sorts, or *devas*. The word *deva* is again a Sanskrit word adopted into English, since the Sanskrit thought developed a vocabulary to fit occult ideas not included in modern European thought, and for which therefore there are no suitable European words. *Deva* is related etymologically to the Latin word *deus* or "god," and to the English word "divine," but in Sanskrit its root meaning is "shining one." The early religious teachers, who apparently sometimes saw these creatures and invented the word, probably were conscious especially of their shining quality, their forms being in a sense "living light." The beings called "angels" in European thought are one type of deva, but we are told that there are many types, and that their true forms are not anthropomorphic. Ordinary students can find out very little about them, because the subject is too advanced and really "occult." (Printed statements which profess to offer details really cannot be checked, being generally based upon subjective clairvoyant impressions.) It is well for even the beginner, however, to be aware of the idea that the occult teaching is that such beings do exist. Even less is known about "elementals." They are said to be of a low degree of development, with no individuality. They are also said to be on the "involutionary" arc of the circle or cycle of development. Thus further development for them lies in the direction of further "involvement" into matter. Although this is correct for them, their influence would thus be "wrong" or "evil" for men. (Certain forms of "black magic" invoke such influence.)

As the "dead" man lives on in the astral world, receiving impressions corresponding to the type of emotion which has been habitual with him during earth life, the astral particles in his sheath (*kamarupa* or "desire body" in Sanskrit) gradually scatter and "evaporate" more and more, until finally there are no longer enough of them left, receiving vibrations, to give a coherent impression from that world. Then, we are told, the man "dies" a second time, in a sense, discarding the final remnants of astral matter. (These, occasionally, may still cohere a little among themselves and form an empty "shell" which will float around aimlessly for a period before its final disintegration—or which might be temporarily appropriated and inhabited by a playful "elemental" which thus might impersonate the man at a spiritualistic seance.) The man himself awakens, after this "second death," to the new and higher world of the *manasic* or mental plane.

The occult teaching is that the real self almost never is attracted to a seance, because it has more interesting and important things to do. If a person has died suddenly, and feels that there is something important which has been left undone, which should be told to some one still alive, he is more likely to try to impress the mind of the other person directly than to try to convey any message through a medium. Sometimes a person who has met with a very sudden and violent death might be looking desperately for a channel of communication, but even in such a case is more likely to be able to impress some close relative or friend, directly. And, as mentioned above, a discarded astral "shell" may be seized and temporarily used, as a kind of "dress-up" costume, by an "elemental," and this is said to account for the trivial and incoherent "messages" sometimes transmitted by mediums. The real man is not in communication, but has gone on into the mental world, but the discarded "shell" retains some impression of some aspects of the personality he had while alive, and thus can sometimes seem to give "proof" of its identity. Also, we are told that there are entities upon the astral levels which correspond to "criminals" in our world (human souls which have repeatedly taken a wrong direction, and which thus may be "trapped" in lower levels for some time), and sometimes they desire very strongly to experience physical sensations once more, and one of these also might seize the opportunity to inhabit temporarily the body of a medium, or of some other psychically sensitive person who is attending the seance. Thus, we are told that attendance upon any kind of mediumistic seance is potentially dangerous, since it might lead to being "possessed" by some other, and evil, individuality. The only correct way to communicate with a beloved dead person is to develop one's own ability to "bring through" the contacts made with him at higher levels, not to expect him to come down again to the physical level.

The mental or *manasic* plane is called *devachan*, or the home of the devas, in Sanskrit, since it is the place where the devas have their real being, even though some of them may possess sheaths of the denser astral material in addition. It is called the "heaven world" in a great deal of modern writing about occultism, since the mental experiences there correspond to the concept of "heaven." The man has discarded everything connected with the earth, or with lower emotions of any type, and now he reaps the results of his highest aspirations, in a mental life of bliss unalloyed, where never even the slightest shadow of fear or sorrow or struggle can penetrate.

According to the outline of devachanic conditions usually given, people whose highest thoughts have connected themselves with their families will see around them "living" images of their loved ones, which will seem real and responsive to them. People who have been interested in philanthropic schemes may construct apparently real Utopias. Scientists will have the opportunity to study some of the real inner laws of nature. Musicians or artists will be aided and taught by the devas who work in those lines, and thus be reborn later with a great enhancement of their capacity. In general, any experience which a man has had of a pure and lofty, or purely intellectual, nature will be worked over and mentally digested, as it were, until he has gained from it the last possible drop of wisdom and enhanced ability. He can have no experience for which there is not some seed already planted—this is not a time for new beginnings, but for gathering together the essence of the past and building it into his permanent self as a permanent part of his character.

We are told that the length of time he spends in *devachan* will depend upon how much of this good material there has been in his past life on earth. The undeveloped or relatively unadvanced person is filled more with emotions which "work out" on the astral plane, and may spend most of the "after-death" life on that plane. A highly evolved person, on the other hand, may spend very little time in the astral world, and many hundreds of years in the mental or "heaven" world. But the relativity of the concept "time" must be borne in mind, remembering how frequently a dream which seems to occupy a very long time is proved to have taken only a few seconds of physical time. Also, there are hints that sometimes an individual who is "on the Path" may be able to "renounce *devachan*," having already during his earthly life distilled his experience into wisdom, and may reincarnate very quickly after physical death. The suggestion seems to be that in such a case he uses the same subtle bodies for the new incarnation as in the preceding one. But this is a mystery.

In the usual case, however, the time comes at last when all of the concrete thoughts and experiences of the past life have been duly wrought over, and again the man drops off any lingering particles of his denser sheath, and now is clad only in the material of the highest subplanes of the *manasic* plane—those subplanes which are called in

Sanskrit the *arupa* or "formless" worlds. The sheath which a man wears at this level has usually been called in English the "causal body," because it contains in itself all the results of the past—not of one life only, but of all the lives which the man has lived since he attained "individualization"—and thus the causes which determine his next life. This "causal body" was formed at the moment of his individualization, and has never been discarded, but has formed the inner nucleus, or highest sheath (inner or highest being material terms really inapplicable to regions of the higher dimensions), of all the many forms he may have worn through the ages. Originally transparent and colorless, like a bubble, serving merely to make a film of separation between this individual and the group consciousness or consciousness of other individuals, it gradually, through many lives, develops the ability to vibrate, as experiences accumulate, and begins to show color. However, we are told, no experience has any real effect upon it except abstract thought or lofty and pure emotions. Bad qualities show here simply as the absence of the corresponding good qualities.

In the highly developed man, this "causal" sheath is a globe of living light, pulsating and radiating, responsive to all the impressions of the higher world, and capable of being used as a vehicle for "spiritual" action. The man will feel himself to be his real Self, at home at his own level. Eventually, he will choose his next incarnation on the basis of what he needs for the next step in his development. A man who is less highly evolved will also supposedly have enough egoic consciousness for his Ego to exert some choice in regard to his next life. (In occult writing, "Ego" means the real Self.) But there are so many blanks in an undeveloped causal body that, after all denser matter has been dropped off, he will be unable to use this finer body as an instrument for receiving impressions, or for really "doing" anything, at the *arupa* or "formless" level. He may be conscious only of a sort of blankness, as though he were lost in a kind of white fog and could not see or hear or "feel" anything. This naturally makes him desire some vehicle more capable of sensation and expression.

This desire leads him back to physical incarnation once more. In his thirst for further experience, he gathers around himself (by a kind of magnetic attraction) material from the lower mental world – corresponding exactly in its quality to the material which he had around him when he "died" before – and then in and around that he gathers material from the astral world, also corresponding in quality to that which surrounded him at the end of his previous life on earth. Thus he will be reborn with the exact capacities for thought and feeling which he deserves, including of course that distilled wisdom which he may have gained when mentally digesting his past experiences in the interval between lives. With his "permanent self" now clad in new mental and astral matter, he is guided to where some physical body is being conceived, which will be of the type his karma requires, both in regard to its physical heredity, and in regard to the type of experience which he will be likely to have in that particular family, among the other individuals with whom he will be related, and with whom he has had other relations in past lives. The "permanent self" or real soul is sexless, and requires incarnations in both sexes, at different times, to give it that balance of experience which will build up a complete and well-rounded or "perfected" individuality. Friends and relatives will meet each other, in life after life, in a variety of different relationships.

This seems to be a good point at which to discuss the matter of memory. The question of why we do not remember our past lives, if we had past lives, may be looked at from either the philosophical or what might be called the "mechanical" aspect. From the "mechanical" point of view, it is quite simple. The memory of other lives is held only in the vehicle of the "permanent self," or "causal body," and when a man reincarnates, he acquires new material for his mental and astral bodies, as well as a new physical brain. The only way in which it would be possible, therefore, for a living individual to remember his past incarnations would be to have some "open" channel of communication between his ordinary brain consciousness and his higher self at the "causal" level. Such a connection is possible, and is one of the goals of occult training, but it is certainly not very common.

The philosophical reason is that it is better to be able to forget the experiences of the past, which have contained many mistakes and the sorrows brought about by those mistakes, and be able to "turn over a new leaf" and start again with a "clean slate." Many a man, at the end of a life full of error and suffering, has seen where some of his mistakes occurred, and sighed "If only I had my life to live over again." Reincarnation offers just that opportunity. If a child of two or three had to remember all the experiences of many past adult lives, there would be little chance for his learning any "new" lessons, or even retaining his sanity.

As to why it would not be better to avoid this rebirth as a baby, and keep one's adult memories and merely live on and on in one continuous life, the analogy of physical growth and evolution shows the answer. If the animals of the Mesozoic had not died, there would be no present-day forms. And we see in many groups of invertebrate animals that there is a recurrent "molting" of the outer body, in order to permit the growth of the form. Any body, even a vertebrate and human one, will inevitably reach a point where it becomes inappropriate for the expanding needs of the consciousness within it. Thus, we continually shed the old form, when it has become stiffened and scarred, and start afresh. But we do remember the real essence of our past lives, and are reborn with the tendencies and abilities we had developed previously—it is only the details which are not ordinarily "brought through."

There have been some cases reported, particularly in countries which accept reincarnation, of children who claimed to remember a previous life, and who seemed able to produce some actual evidence of such memory. This would be possible if, for some karmic reason, the individual reincarnated quite quickly after death, using the same astral and mental bodies as before, instead of spending a long time in the subtle worlds and discarding these bodies and then acquiring new ones just before rebirth. In this case, the memory of the life just past would be more readily accessible, because it would be retained in the astral and mental bodies. All of the memories are retained at the higher level, but in most cases it is better not to have them intruding upon the new business at hand, and to retain only the essential guidelines of conscience and innate abilities. When an individual has made sufficient progress "on the Path," then he may be able to make connections which will permit the memory of past lives, but he will open up such memories only for some special reason.

The normal individual, passing through death, lives for a time in the subtle worlds, and then, finding himself still really unequipped for life in purely spiritual regions, returns once more to physical life to add to his experiences. Again and again he lives and dies and lives again, each time a little farther along the way toward the goal. When he reaches that goal, earthly life will be no longer necessary for him.

CHAPTER X

THE BASIC IDEA OF THE GOAL OF LIFE

We know we are alive. That was our first proposition. But, as self-conscious, evolving units of life, there is some urge in our inner selves which makes us want to know why we are alive. What are we supposed to do about it, now that we are here? Can we find out the real goal of life, its basic purpose?

We may as well admit in the first place that concerning the ultimate beginning and ending we know nothing, and can know nothing at our present stage. Why there is a manifested universe at all we cannot know. It lies with the One Unknowable which is in and behind and beyond everything. Out of Its inscrutable Being, universes come into being and pass away again, and we can no more understand Its ultimate purposes than one atom in one cell of our bodies can understand our purposes – perhaps not even so much. But the great Teacher who was called the Enlightened One – the Buddha – pointed out very truly that men do not need to know the ultimates. What they need is very simple – merely the knowledge of the next step, with some view of the successive steps on the path. As we go forward, our vision widens, as when a man climbing a mountain sees farther and farther as he mounts higher.

For very simple people, a simple ethical teaching, which will help them to know which way is forward, is more important than the giving out of teaching which they are as yet unable to understand. But we may be sure that the teaching recorded in the Buddhist scriptures, given in public sermons by the Buddha, and intended for the "little ones," although so beautiful in its clarity and simplicity, was not the whole of his teaching. Buddhism also had, and has, its esoteric side, its occult knowledge available only to those whose spiritual advancement has prepared them for it. However, since many of the ideas which used to be purely "esoteric" or secret have been given out to the Western world in the past century, we are now able to avail ourselves of a great deal of that Wisdom which has been preserved down through the ages. So, perhaps, for those who seek correctly, it may be possible to understand that segment of the great Plan which concerns our human evolution, at least.

Within what H. P. Blavatsky calls the "Ring-pass-not" of our system – that portion of space-time which constitutes our "universe" and concerning which we are able to form any concept at all – we find certain great laws in operation. One of the most fundamental of these seems to be that the infinite and boundless consciousness of the One Life, on the highest conceivable plane, seeks to enrich itself by dividing itself into many separate units of consciousness, pouring itself down into matter and form in order that these units of consciousness may have experience and growth and become each an image of the Whole, and then resolving them back once more into the great Whole at a higher turn of the spiral.

Herbert Spencer had some glimpse of this when he formulated his famous theory of a universe gradually differentiating more and more into a greater number of separate, distinct parts. But he failed to grasp the complete law of cycles according to which the separated parts combine once more into larger organized and integrated units, and then into higher and more inclusive groups or integrated units, and at the completion of one turn of the great Wheel – one outbreathing and indrawing of the Great Breath – are all once more one with the One.

In this great process of involution and evolution, man stands midway. In the consciousness of mankind we find the greatest development of the process of differentiation, that point where the sense of separated individuality reaches its climax, and where we find the beginnings of a higher type of group consciousness, in which the essential individuality is not negated, but, enriched by the experience gained in the separation, enriches the Whole thereby. Having faced outward and downward for many ages, for every man there comes a time when he takes the Path of Return: "When that which drew from out the boundless deep, Turns again home."

We thus find that the goal of individual human life falls into two categories, according to whether the man in question has or has not yet reached that point of climax and turning.

Life is a school for souls, and in that school there are many different grades, and the lessons for one grade are not the same as the lessons for another grade. That is where so many Christians, who have lost touch with the old Wisdom, make a great mistake. They assume that there is one teaching which is suitable for all men, that there are such things as absolute good and absolute evil, and that rules can be laid down according to which all men may know which is the evil they should avoid and which the good they should seek. There are no such absolutes. What is "right" for each man depends upon his own particular stage of development, and the direction of his growth at that particular time.

The older religions were wiser in giving out one teaching for simple men, and reserving for "initiates," pledged to secrecy, the teaching suitable for higher grades of evolution. The higher teaching was always individualized, too. Every now and then, down through the ages, we have had some highly advanced man who, by his own effort, had found some aspect of this higher teaching (or who perhaps broke some vow of secrecy because of misguided compassion and desire to hasten the evolution of the younger souls), and who gave out some fragment of formerly "esoteric" teaching to the multitudes. Even though such teaching may have been helpful to a few, all too often it has but served to make "confusion worse confounded" in the minds of those who were not experienced enough to be prepared for it. The greatest Teachers—the actual great

Founders of the great religions—were usually very careful to adapt their words to the understanding of their listeners, but their disciples were not always so wise, and every religion has become perverted and distorted, within a generation or so from the death of its Founder, by the inability of its followers to use due discrimination.

There are no absolute, set rules for human behavior. For one man, who has lived many lives and had the opportunity to gain wisdom from them, many things may be "wrong" which are natural and normal for the less evolved man. There is no uniformity in human nature. We do not expect from a little child the same self-control and consideration for others that we expect from a civilized adult. If we are wise and have some understanding of psychology, we know that children need rough-and-tumble play, and the kind of knowledge which can be gained only by experience, and independent development of strength. We do not expect them to behave like "little ladies and gentlemen" in early childhood. We have even discovered that those few children who do behave themselves in this supposedly exemplary manner are psychologically inadequate when they are grown. They have no strength, no character, no will of their own. If they had been "bad" a little as children, they would make better adults.

So it is in that larger cycle of growth which is a complete human life—which includes many "lives" on earth and periods of intervening life in the subtle worlds. It is foolish to preach to, and try to force upon, undeveloped individuals —whether in primitive cultures or in the lower levels of "civilized" life—the same rules of conduct which awaken spiritual aspirations in more highly evolved men. All the ethical teaching such individuals need is that each action brings its appropriate result, because all men are somehow parts of a greater whole, and therefore attempts to lift themselves by pushing down other men really *will not work,* but mutual comradeship and cooperation will achieve results faster. Those who are somewhat more intelligent need to be taught that to think is the outstanding human ability, and to think better and more rationally is the next step.

First things must come first, and in general men's bodies must be reasonably strong and well, properly nourished and free from disease, before their minds can expand. Next comes the proper development of the emotions, through the right kind of emotional experience with family and friends, and the refining of the esthetic sensitivities. Third comes mental development, and those who are farther advanced should try to help the younger souls to develop intellectually, training their minds to think clearly and truthfully, and teaching them true facts about the world and about themselves, without dogmatism or authoritarianism, but clearing away misconceptions. For those who are still "imprisoned in ignorance and superstition," it is worse than useless to preach dogmatically and literally the lofty ethical ideals set forth by the great religious teachers of mankind for their close disciples.

In the early days of humanity, there were not many bodies available, in which to incarnate, at any one time. Thus there were differences in the dates at which individualization became possible. Human progress was very slow. Crude stone tools date back at least two million years, pottery making and agriculture only eight or ten thousand years, while city life began in only a very few places several thousand years later.* Therefore individual egos probably had very long periods between incarnations. With the recent increase in world population, we must have many individuals in incarnation now who have had very little, if any, experience of civilized life. At the same time we may have a special influx of a great many who are much "older." The very young ones must have freedom for growth and development, but must not be allowed to become too destructive, for their own sake as well as for that of others.

---

* These datings are given here according to the latest findings of archeological science. However, many theosophical writers and other students of occult philosophy prefer to accept the traditions in regard to Atlantis and other ancient civilizations which have supposedly disappeared beneath the seas.

Yet they should not be considered "inferior," but merely younger. Human brotherhood is very precious and very real, and souls of different ages may incarnate sometimes even in the same family.

Most human beings are still on the "Path of Outgoing." What they need most is to act, and to acquire knowledge of the results of action, through their own individual experience of all the fullness of living, and thus to develop their understanding, rather than to stagnate and merely accept the ideas of priests or other supposed authorities. Even if they make mistakes, and do things which bring unpleasant results upon themselves, so long as they do not interfere with the growth and development of others, they may still be making progress in learning discrimination, and in that sense doing right. They need to learn things for themselves, by acting for themselves, and exploring the potentialities for growth in any and all directions. They need to develop minds capable of independent thought, capable of analyzing experiences and rejecting superstition. No one is ready for the "Path of Return" until he has learned for himself, in the school of repeated lives, which kinds of actions bring the happiness of harmonious growth, and which kinds bring the opposite, and that love and cooperation are really more helpful to himself than hatred and aggressiveness. He cannot learn this from precepts, but only from personal experience. Also, he needs to develop his intellect until it is a keen and accurate instrument of thought, capable of sifting evidence and reaching valid conclusions independently, before trying to develop the faculties which lie beyond intellect. Reason is what distinguishes mankind from other mammals, and further development of reason is what the human race as a whole needs most at the present time.

Perhaps the need for spiritual enlightenment is the greatest for those who stand at the turning point. Many men have reached a high level of intellectual development and individual awareness at the present period. Several thousand years ago, only a handful of men in each generation reached the point where they needed more than simple ethical rules, and for them there were the mystery schools of the various religions. Now there are too many people at that stage of development to be handled in the old individual way, and that is one reason why much of the knowledge formerly esoteric or occult has in the last century been intentionally revealed, and may be found in books by those who know how to seek and read and understand.

After many lives of killing and being killed, getting and spending, loving and hating, the time comes to every man when he finds that there is no permanent satisfaction in earthly things. Possessions lose their value once they are acquired, sensations lose their taste when indulged in too freely. Even intellectual attainment begins to seem purposeless. Then it is that the man reaches the turning point, and, though he may for a while hesitate and linger and doubt, because the change in direction will mean a complete reversal of all of his previous habits, an inner homesickness of the soul drives him on until he turns, like the Prodigal Son of the parable, and sets his face toward home and his Father's house. Up to this point, everything he has done which has heightened his sense of separateness and individuality (without injuring others) has been good and right for him. Now he must work in the opposite direction, and begin to gain the sense of unity, to realize that the separateness of his little personal self is really an illusion, and the One Self is the only reality.

The Buddha spoke of the way of escape from the Wheel of Rebirth. The Hindu religion speaks of the ultimate goal of Liberation. The Christian speaks of salvation. All of these really mean the same thing – that a time will come when all of the earth lessons will be learned. Then the man will enter the spiritual kingdom, the "Kingdom of Heaven," which is just as real, and just as truly one of the great kingdoms of Nature, as the preceding mineral, vegetable, animal, and human kingdoms. (Occultists consider the human kingdom to be a fourth kingdom, not part of the animal kingdom.) Beyond the human lies the super-human or fifth kingdom. And the goal for the evolution of man, in this present world system, covering many millions of years, is the achievement of that state of development which will make it possible for him to come into his heritage and enter that kingdom.

When each man first attained individualization, there was formed around him a subtle sheath called sometimes the "causal body," which became the real vehicle for his separated individuality, and which has remained the center or focus of his being all through the many incarnations into earthly life. Gradually this sheath (made of material of the "higher mental" levels) becomes more radiant and vibrant until it is a perfect vehicle for experience at its own level. But when the time comes for the man to transcend humanity, then this sheath in turn must be dropped, as his successive physical bodies have been dropped before, and his consciousness will awaken on a higher plane, known as the "intuitional" or *buddhic* level, where there is no longer any barrier or film of separation, but each center of consciousness feels itself one with the Whole.

Yet there is no loss of essential individuality, because all the long experience of earthly lives has formed so strong a center that it can still maintain its focus, and know and experience from its own center, even when its circumference expands to include the whole "plane," and is, as it were, superimposed upon countless other circumferences. Each spirit has its own center, and retains the memory of all its past human lives, yet knows itself one with the rest, and somehow shares in their memories too. This is a condition which is really indescribable in words, and beyond our powers of comprehension, but we are told that this is as near the truth as we can come, and that it is this which is meant by the esoteric teachings of all religions when they speak of the aspiration for "unity" or "union with the One," as an actual and abiding achievement rather than in the sense of the emotion felt briefly during moments of mystic exaltation.

We must remember, however, that evolution proceeds by progressive development, step by step. Those philosophies which teach that it is possible to achieve unity, enlightenment, or salvation, in some miraculous manner, and jump from the condition of ordinary humanity, full of faults and failings, to the state of perfect bliss and achievement, all in a moment, merely by reorienting oneself and undergoing some mystical experience — and thenceforth to have no further need for life on earth — are sheer nonsense. It is true that the reorientation is necessary, but it is only the first step. After that, the man has entered the "Path of Return," but the way still lies ahead of him — the ladder of spiritual evolution is still to be climbed.

Many virtues must be built into the character, patiently, painstakingly, and permanently. Many faults and impurities must be done away with, as impediments to progress. The Buddhists call such faults "fetters," and list ten chief ones which must be utterly and completely cast off, one by one. The steps of the "Noble Eightfold Path" represent the positive requirements. As the man works and strives, and begins to climb a little above the general mass, he finds that there are others who have climbed ahead of him, who stretch down to him helping hands, and impart to him the teaching he needs when he is ready for it.

At certain very advanced stages of progress, he comes to crises where he undergoes certain expansions of consciousness which are known, in occult terminology, as "initiations." A great number of lives would normally be spent between one initiation and the next, but for any man who has decided to take the steeper "Occult Path," it is possible to hasten considerably the normal course of evolution. After the Fourth Great Initiation, a man is technically known as an "Arhat." Another, Fifth Initiation, makes him an "Adept," for whom nothing in the three worlds of human evolution (the physical, astral, and mental planes) remains unknown or out of reach. This is the goal of all merely human evolution. All men will reach this level one day, but for many this may be not until millions of years have passed. Some few have always pressed ahead of their fellows, however, and it is those who have thus achieved, yet still remain on earth to help their younger brothers, who constitute the "Inner Government of the World"—the "Occult Hierarchy"—the "Great White Lodge" of Masters of the Wisdom.

CHAPTER XI

THE BASIC IDEA OF THE BROTHERHOOD WHICH WATCHES OVER THE WORLD

The occult concept of Masters or Mahatmas seems very strange at first to the person who has known only Christian or materialistic ideas. But it is an old concept perfectly familiar to past civilizations, and it can be shown also that it is quite in harmony with the scientific ideas of progress and evolution. (The Sanskrit word *Mahatma* means, literally, "great spirit." The title was applied to Gandhi, but only in this general sense, rather than in the sense in which it is used technically in the study of occultism.)

One of the differences between what is ordinarily called "mysticism" and what is here called "occultism" is in regard to this concept of Masters. The man who calls himself a mystic generally thinks of his own self as in direct relation to some ultimate divine Self. Much of his thinking is intuitive and unsystematic, incompletely verbalized, or expressed in allegorical form because it really cannot be verbalized. The occultist (as the term is used here) has the concept of a Hierarchy of developed or perfected men, who have real and tested knowledge concerning the things of the spirit, and among whom he aspires to take his place some day. The occult student therefore attempts to organize his knowledge, as well as purify himself, and to prepare himself to become a pupil of one of the members of the Hierarchy. He believes that this Hierarchy has been in continual existence since the earliest days of mankind.

In the beginning, the leaders of the Occult Hierarchy on this earth are said to have been mighty beings whose evolution had been completed upon some other globe, who came here to guide and lead infant humanity. Later, as some earth humans became competent to take their place, these early "God-Kings" withdrew. Various lines of development were followed in different parts of the world, during different ages, but always there was an Inner Wisdom (behind the outer, exoteric religions) which was in the possession of the higher members of the Hierarchy, and access to which was, in former ages, to be gained through a long period of training in some mystery religion. Whatever the outer religion might be, the inner, esoteric teaching was given only to those trained and tested and able to understand it. Possibly some of the great sages and prophets of the Old Testament, or some of the saints of the centuries of the Christian era, were men who had taken the Occult Path, and who actually had access to some aspects of this Inner Wisdom, in varying degrees. But it was never possible for such knowledge to be revealed openly to the multitudes.

As the centuries passed, and ritualism and materialism accumulated side by side, as the world progressed from ancient to modern times, more and more attention was paid to material things, and fewer and fewer aspirants to occult teaching were to be found in the outer world. The Wisdom was kept in its purity only in hidden, sheltered places — in the deserts or in hidden mountain valleys. There the custodians of the Wisdom kept the torch alight, handing it on only to those very few who somehow found access to them, who in turn passed it on to later followers. Through the long centuries they waited, watching for that tide in the affairs of men when the race would be ready for a new step of spiritual progress, and many men would have attained that level of development at which it would be possible for them to take the first occult step. That point was reached during the past century, and the messengers of the Wisdom began to appear, to tell us that the Wisdom still exists, and the Masters are waiting for us to come to them.

There is no way to "prove" the existence of Masters — men who are "perfected," so far as merely human progress is concerned. No individual who has had some personal experience which brings him conviction can possibly pass on that experience or that conviction to others. But if civilized man has evolved from animal-man, is it not logical to believe that there may be a higher evolution, beyond that of the normal present day? And since we know that different people learn and progress at quite different rates, is it not conceivable that those who were the greatest and wisest men of past ages, if their souls decided that speed of development was both necessary and desirable, would have been able to get so far ahead of the average by now as to be quite beyond ordinary comprehension? Of course, this assumes acceptance of the doctrine of reincarnation and the continuity of individual souls throughout successive lives of progressive development. But it is to be hoped that the reader who has reached this point has accepted this basic doctrine, at least tentatively, since it is so utterly basic and necessary that without it there can be no real comprehension of the occult teaching.

The Masters, then, are men who decided, each one individually, at some far distant period of the past, after they had entered the Path of Return, that they would follow the steeper way of the "Occult Path," and progress as rapidly as possible, far beyond the rate of ordinary men, in order to achieve the goal far sooner and be able then to help the younger souls. All of our struggles, all of our sufferings, they have known and undergone, and overcome, in lives of intensified experience, until they reached that peak of achievement which the average man will not reach until the end of the present system. Some men who reach that point pass out of reach of mankind altogether, although they also serve the great scheme of evolution, in ways beyond our power to understand, but the Masters are those who, reaching that point, elected to turn back, and reincarnate into fleshly bodies again, though the need for such limitation was past for them, in order to serve as guides and teachers of the race.

Ever and anon, through the ages, one of the Masters has come forth out of retirement, to give out to the world some part of the Wisdom which seemed useful for a particular race of mankind. These have been the Founders of the world's great religions. According to one tradition, he who became the Buddha had been the Founder of a succession of religions for earlier peoples, in previous lives in other lands, being remembered later only in myth or legend. In his last life on earth, he became the "Enlightened One," the Buddha, and when he died, passed into *Paranirvana,* having gone so far beyond the level even of the highest Masters as to enter the formless region beyond space and time, from which there is no return to earthly life. Then (according to this tradition) his place as World Teacher was taken by another Great One, in the office of Bodhisattva, or "Buddha-to-be." The Buddhists call him the Lord Maitreya, who will be the "Buddha of Compassion" (Gautama having been the "Buddha of Wisdom"), and some students of occultism say that, although at present he is using only subtle vehicles, without a dense physical body, he is in very truth the "Teacher of angels and of men," who will come forth into the world again and yet again for future races. One tradition identifies him with Krishna of Hindu legend and with the Christian idea of the indwelling Christ.

Some people who have heard of the idea of Masters think of them always as Orientals, but occultists who have reason to know whereof they speak say that all races of men are represented among the Hierarchy. Some who lived in the Himalayan Mountains at the time of H. P. Blavatsky permitted their names to be revealed, and certain facts to be given out about them, because they were sufficiently secluded by the then nearly impassable mountains to be free, in their physical bodies, from intrusion by curiosity-seekers. (We have had no really authentic reports about these particular Masters in later years, although many pseudo-occult groups claim present-day telepathic contact with them.) But there are said to be others who live in Western countries, leading quiet and secluded lives, which are inconspicuous and apparently normal. Their private contacts with other members of the Hierarchy would be carried on by telepathy, or in their subtle bodies, with no need for physical means of communication.

Although they have physical bodies (as a sort of fulcrum for exertion of energy), most of the work of the Masters is said to be done at mental levels, sometimes while they are awake, but often also with their bodies in deep repose or trance. (This habit, combined with purity of life, enables them to use the same physical body for a longer than average number of years.) At any moment, a Master can focus his consciousness upon any spot of the globe, and enter into the inner consciousness of any living being, if he so desires. He can read the thoughts of any man, and if that man be sufficiently sensitive to impressions from his own higher self, the Master can impress certain ideas upon him. It is in this way that the great leaders of mankind, in various fields of achievement, receive so-called "inspiration." Some men are disciples of the Masters, and receive instruction and enlightenment from them while they are asleep, and functioning in the subtle worlds. Even though, when they awake, their physical brain may not remember just how the ideas came to them, the new ideas are there to be used.

A very few pupils have really learned to "link up" their physical brains with their higher selves, and for them it is possible to know and remember the contact they may have had with their Master. Some of them have written books, presenting some of the actual words spoken to them by the Master. In the nature of the case, no list of titles can be attempted. All that can be said is that such books do exist, and can be found and studied, and that for the student who is spiritually ready, the fact that the words come from a Master will seem evident as he reads. (He should never accept testimony about this from any one else, without his own inner feeling of certainty.) But there must be much preliminary study, and that development which comes only from unselfish service to the race, over a long period, before such teachings can be identified or understood.

Most of the books which deal with the idea of Masters are outrageously fictional.

Because of this ability to influence the minds of men, both individually and in the mass, the Occult Hierarchy is sometimes known as the Inner Government of the World. However, not even a Master can interfere with man's free power of choice. From them come impressions and suggestions, which men feel without recognizing their source, but it is the man himself who decides how he will act. And when men *will* to act in wrong and selfish ways, they reap the karmic results, and all the love and compassion of the Masters is powerless to interfere. The doctrine of "vicarious atonement" was invented by people who knew nothing of occult law, and is quite irrational—and unnecessary in the light of the ideas of karma and reincarnation. "No man can purify another. All the Buddhas merely point the way."

The Masters are sometimes called the Elder Brothers, and we are told it is thus that they like to have us think of them. They know and understand all our weaknesses and our sorrows, because they have gone through it all before, but instead of passing on into the bliss and radiance of higher spheres, they have lingered in order to pour forth upon us waves of love and courage and enlightenment which may help us to know the Way and follow it with less stumbling. They are not mysterious angelic beings, forever inaccessible, but truly human in every way, hard as it may be for us to imagine a perfected human being. If we seek them, and long to become their disciples, we must remember that they know us and watch us long before we can become aware of them, and they stand waiting and eager to receive us. Only, they cannot come down to our level— this would be too great a waste of energy—we must train ourselves until we can make contact with theirs. Every true disciple is welcomed by them, because their task is very heavy, as they watch over all the fumbling of humanity, and every advanced soul who helps his younger brothers is helping to lighten their load also.

CHAPTER XII

THE BASIC IDEA OF THE OCCULT PATH

To serious students of occultism, the term "the Occult Path" is one not to be spoken lightly, as the Path itself is one not lightly to be entered upon. Sometimes the word "Path" is used alone, with no explanation of its meaning, but in occult terminology it has very definite implications, and no discussion of the basic ideas of occult teaching would be complete without some explanation of this most important concept. The deeper implications, however, can be grasped only in proportion to one's own actual progress "on the Path."

As was explained previously, for every soul there comes a time for reversal of direction, leaving the Path of Outgoing and starting back upon the Path of Return. The upward progress thereafter, for most men, is slow and gradual, like the ascent of a mountain by a winding road, by which, in due time, the top may be reached. But there are always a few individuals who, catching a view of the summit, try to break out a new route up the face of the cliff. The Occult Path represents such a steep ascent, by which progress may be immeasurably accelerated. But it is hazardous and full of difficulties, and, once the choice has been made, and the more direct ascent attempted, there is no way to get back to the slower path.

The decision to enter the Occult Path is made, with deliberate intent, by the man's "permanent" Higher Self, which thereby undertakes to "balance" past karma, and to pay off any karmic debts that may have been incurred in the past, and which still remain unpaid, as rapidly as possible. This may result in conditions very unpleasant to the lower, personal self – physical illness or imperfection, poverty, loneliness, or other problems. The personality, at the level of physical brain consciousness, may not realize that such a decision has been made, and may sometimes wonder why it is subjected to so many trials and difficulties, while other men, who seem to deserve less, seem to be happy and prosperous. This bewilderment is usually only temporary, however, and is more likely to occur while the physical body is still rather young, and the higher Self has not yet gained much control over the lower vehicles. As the man matures, ever striving toward what he feels is right, yielding not to discouragement, but pressing steadily onward, the time comes when he realizes the purpose of it all. He may make some conscious connection between his physical brain and his higher Self, or he may meet with some companion on the Path who will bring him once more into touch with the old Wisdom which he has already known in previous lives. No one ever struggles unwatched, or really alone. Always those on the "inner planes" are aware of the progress made, and are ready to help when karma permits.

One may wonder how it is possible for a highly evolved man, who is ready for the Occult Path, to have any appreciable amount of adverse karma still hanging over him. How is it that he has done things wrong enough to deserve so much trouble? The explanation lies in the fact that unevolved men make so many blunders that it is impossible to adjust them all quickly. If the weight of their total adverse karma were allowed to fall back immediately on young souls, they would be too weak to bear it and still make any progress. Therefore the heaviest part of the load is somehow held back until the soul has grown and developed strength, when it can begin to work out the karmic adjustments, gradually. At the ordinary rate of progress, these would be spread out over so many lives as to be comparatively easy to bear. It is only the urge for speed on the Path which brings about a relatively heavy dose in a short space of time.

The stages of the Path are described rather completely in old Hindu and Buddhist literature, and the Western student will find a good many modern books which attempt to summarize them and present the old teachings in modern language. In all of these writings, the very first step on the Path is given as "right discrimination." This means the ability to distinguish between the "real" and the "unreal," to understand which things pertain to the real higher Self and which only to the lower temporary personality. When this distinction is made, the trials and tribulations which may result from adverse karma lose their power to produce real unhappiness. The man realizes that his body is only a temporary overcoat, and that the things which happen to it cannot harm his real Self. Many apparently adverse conditions can be utilized as experiences from which to learn.

The shifting of the focus of attention from lower to higher levels occurs gradually. That is, it may take a very long time before the focus can be kept steadily at the higher level. Results are achieved most effectively by some definite method of training, rather than by leaving it all to chance or sporadic and random efforts. Different methods are suitable for people of different temperaments, and in different races or periods of civilization. The word "yoga," which is much misused at present, orginally meant such a method, a way to achieve a junction or union between the brain consciousness and the higher Self. (The word "yoga" derives from the same root as these words.) When this connection or linking-up can be made and maintained, then the shift of attention, and identification with the higher aspect, can be achieved. But a long period of sustained and steady effort is indispensable.

There are many different types of yoga, each using a distinct method, and originally intended for a specific purpose. The student can find more detailed treatment elsewhere. Only a definition of the terms used to name them will be offered here for most of these systems.

Mantra yoga uses special combinations of sounds, called *mantras*, to produce subtle and psychological effects. If given by a teacher who is enough of an adept to perceive these subtle effects, it is said that astonishing results may sometimes be achieved. Laya yoga deals with the inner "fires" of the body, and can be extremely dangerous. (See what was said about the chakras at the end of chapter IV.) Hatha yoga consists primarily of various practices for the purification and control of the physical body. Some of these can also be dangerous. Some of the advanced Sanskrit texts on Hatha yoga give techniques of meditation, but these are directed to the premature development of the physical and psychical centers, and the powers acquired by these means, without sufficient attention to the mental, emotional, or ethical aspects, may lead to dangers.

Various modification of Hatha yoga are what most of the books on yoga now published and available in the West are dealing with. Most of these are advertised as offering a way to achieve health and youth. Although some of the exercises may be useful for physical training, many books also contain some quite unsuited to Occidental bodies. Many of the practices are really intended to train the consciousness to become aware of, and gain control over, functions usually governed by the sympathetic nervous system, which it would be better to leave to the efficient automatism of the body. This type of Hatha yoga exercise represents a reversal, or turning against the flow of evolution. It is not only pointless and a waste of time, but, we are told, persistent practice may bring rather devastating consequences, to mind or body, or both. But it is possible to find books which include only those exercises which are safe, if instructions are followed with sufficient care. In general, any system which stresses what might be called physical "stunts" of very peculiar type should be avoided.

The three systems mentioned so far are not even mentioned in some discussions of yoga, which deal with only the four main types. These are Karma yoga, Bhakti yoga, Jñana yoga, and Raja yoga.

Karma yoga is discussed in the *Bhagavad-Gita*. It deals with achievement by right action, and the *Gita* points out that right action should not be undertaken for the sake of its "fruits," or results, but solely for its own sake. Bhakti yoga is also dealt with in the *Gita* (as well as in many other works). This is the yoga of love or devotion, by which the focus of consciousness is shifted away from the personal self. The lower self may be transcended through intense love for some ideal, usually thought of as a personal incarnation of diety, although any self-forgetfulness through love is a form of Bhakti yoga. Jñana yoga is the yoga of pure reason or Wisdom. It is sometimes said to correspond to philosophy (in the Western sense). The power of the mind is employed in reflection upon such questions as the true nature of the "I." By this type of meditation the lower mind may, in time, be stilled and transcended, and the level of "intuition" reached. The classic Sanskrit work on this is the *Viveka Chudamani,* by Shankaracharya, the title of which is often translated as "The Crest Jewel of Wisdom" or "The Crest Jewel of Discrimination." But there are also other works which can be studied. Each of these three systems appeals to a different kind of temperament.

Raja yoga, as indicated by its name, which means the "kingly yoga," is sometimes said to be the highest type of yoga, but it may also be considered simply as the yoga suited for a still different temperament. Meditation is also the method used here, but the emphasis is upon use of the will, or intense effort and exertion. These are naturally to be applied at very high levels, ultimately. Raja yoga is outlined succinctly (and enigmatically) by the great Sanskrit writer Patanjali, in a book called the *Yoga-Sutras.* The original is a series of not quite two hundred short sentences or aphorisms, the meaning of which is extremely obscure. These were probably, originally, intended to be memorized merely as cues to more extensive discussions. At any rate, almost since the days of Patanjali himself (probably three or four centuries before the Christian era), the work has always been presented with the accompaniment of extensive commentaries or explanations. There have probably been at least a score of English translations of the verses published, each with a somewhat different interpretation. One of the most recent, by I. K. Taimni, called *The Science of Yoga*,* seems to the writer to be far superior to any others she has studied. Not only are the individual Sanskrit words explained, but the extensive comments seem to indicate a much deeper knowledge of the real occult wisdom contained in the original work.

It is said that, for actual practice of the Patanjali system, as distinguished from mere intellectual study of the philosophy, the student should be under the constant watchfulness of an already advanced living guru (teacher), who can check and make sure that the practices of the pupil are being done really correctly. Such a guru is not readily obtainable by any Westerner. But it should be pointed out, also, that the instructions of Patanjali were intended for students already quite advanced in the study of occultism, and he outlines many preliminary conditions which must be fulfilled before undertaking the actual meditation exercises.

It might be well here to mention some of these preliminary conditions. They are sometimes spoken of as the eight "limbs" or parts of yoga. The first is self-restraint, in five respects. There must be abstention from violence, from falsehood, from theft, from incontinence, and from acquisitiveness. Then there must be observances, also given with five subdivisions. These are purity (elimination from the body, emotions, and mind, of all elements which might impede the proper functioning of these vehicles of the Self), contentment (in order not to let the self be disturbed by reactions to external stimuli), austerity (self-discipline), self-study, and self-surrender. Each of these really requires extensive commentaries to explain them, and any one might take a lifetime to achieve in complete form. Further requirements follow, those mentioned so far constituting merely the first two out of the eight! Mention is also made of certain "hindrances" which need first to be attenuated, and then completely done away with, before one can expect to

* The Theosophical Publishing House

achieve even the first stage of *samadhi,* of which there are many stages.

The first of the hindrances mentioned in the Patanjali system is *avidya.* This literally means "ignorance," but the implications of the word are vast. It means the lack of awareness of Reality, susceptibility to illusion, and much else. In the Buddhist listing, *avidya* is the last of the faults to be overcome. The second hindrance, according to Patanjali, is the sense of egoism, or "I-am-ness." Buddhism refers to the delusion of the separateness of the self. Further hindrances are: attractions, repulsions, and strong desire for life. In other words, in order to practice, adequately, the Patanjali type of meditation which leads to the various stages of *samadhi,* one must have overcome the tendency to violent emotional reactions of any type, either positive or negative, and be able to look upon everything coolly and objectively. Yet, after some of these preliminaries have been attended to, and real meditation is begun, there is an emphasis upon love and compassion.

All of this has been mentioned here merely to point out to the reader that yoga involves a great deal more than could ever be guessed merely from perusal of some of the modern books bearing that title. Real yoga, by whatever method, is not a system for bodily development, but is aimed at stilling or quieting the jumping-about of the mind, so that impressions from the higher levels may be able to penetrate through the mental and emotional levels and come into the brain consciousness.

Naturally, the emotional self must also be purified and rendered calm. The analogy is sometimes given of physical reflection. Light cast on moving water will not reflect a true image, and the nature of the emotional or astral body is considered to be analogous to that of water. The mind is sometimes considered, metaphorically, to be like a mirror. It may reflect or picture things which are impressed on it by the reports of the physical sense organs, or feelings impressed on it by the emotional self, but it may also be turned or focused in such a way as to reflect impressions from the higher self. But light cannot be reflected from a mirror which is clouded, and if the mind is full of all kinds of imagery from lower levels, and the thoughts continually jump around, no true impression from higher levels can be made. Therefore, concentration is a necessary preliminary to meditation, and meditation, in occult literature, is preliminary to *samadhi*. This is sometimes translated as "contemplation," but really stands for a state of mind which is so far beyond ordinary meditation that it probably cannot be really understood except by some one who has experienced it. The word "trance" is sometimes used as a translation, but trance implies an absence of consciousness, and *samadhi* is said to be, instead, a more intensified kind of consciousness, although it does not involve images in the normal sense. And there are, furthermore, various levels of *samadhi*.

Many books have been published in recent years which outline methods of meditation, and probably a great many of them could be helpful to beginners. But most of these books are written from the point of view of the general usefulness of meditation, in helping one in daily life or business, and have little to do with occult training or aspirations for progress on the Path. Apart from the strictly theosophical publications on the subject, which of course do have the occult viewpoint, the books of Paul Brunton seem to be a noteworthy exception to the general rule, being definitely intended to offer suggestions to those who are in search of what he calls the "Overself." Although Brunton apparently had no connection with the specifically theosophical traditions, his best works seem to show that he had been in touch with some one really initiated into the Wisdom. Such, at least, is the impression made on the present writer.

Some people seem to believe that they can obtain contact with some higher self, or with what they call intuition, by some heightening of the emotions. Although in a sense this is what is done by Bhakti yoga, it is also necessary to point out that real intuition is never contrary to reason, but represents a higher form of reasoning, carried on more rapidly in the higher mind, and quite distinct from the impressions which may come from the emotional self, or what in ordinary psychology is referred to as the subconscious mind, full of all kinds of confused ideas. The most important lesson for the average civilized individual of today to learn is that permitting actions to be controlled by emotion, or impulse, is unworthy of any adult member of the species *Homo sapiens*. Far too many people consider it normal and right to do what they "feel like" doing, instead of stopping to think before they act, and use their reason. To be sure, it is desirable to have the right kind of emotions, but even the finest emotions are not trustworthy guides to action. Action should be based upon mature and rational judgment as to what its results are likely to be. To quote the chief character in the science fiction novel *Stranger in a Strange Land,* by Robert A. Heinlein, "Goodness is not enough, goodness is never enough. . . . A hard, cold wisdom is required for goodness to accomplish good."

This is merely a modern way of emphasizing the need for the quality which the occult books call *vairagya,* sometimes translated as desirelessness, but really meaning "dispassion." Very few people in the world at present can really think clearly at all. Some few can think clearly and dispassionately when they are not tired, or hungry, or disturbed emotionally by some problem. But the aim of the man who aspires to take the next step in human progress should be to learn to think clearly and dispassionately, steadily, all the time.

Before leaving the subject of the various kinds of yoga, it might be well to mention the books on what is called Agni yoga. The name means the yoga of fire, and the contents of the books in this series indicate that the teachings are meant chiefly for individuals who are now preparing for the new type of humanity. They are rather incomprehensible unless one has already made considerable occult progress, but contain many stimulating and poetic ideas. The reader can judge them only on the basis of his own insight and own personal sense of response or recognition. Agni yoga is mentioned here only to make the list more complete, since it is newer than the traditional types of yoga, while at the same time being very definitely addressed to students on the Path.

The purpose of any system of occult training or yoga is, or should be, to help to achieve some sort of connection between the brain consciousness and the real spiritual Self, in order that illumination gained upon spiritual levels may be made available for use at physical levels. Sometimes, in the course of such training, the consciousness awakens also to sights and sounds which originate upon astral or lower mental levels, but this type of awareness, which is usually called psychic ability, is not, and never should be, a thing to be sought for its own sake. If the "powers" (as they are occultly called—*siddhis* in Sanskrit) come naturally and normally, in the course of spiritual development, they can be controlled and handled as useful tools. But if they are developed by special methods, prematurely, their unfortunate possessor is more likely to achieve insanity than any high development! There are forces existent upon astral and mental levels which are far more dangerous to meddle with, without an adequate technique, than a high voltage wire!

Thousands of years ago, when real occult training was available in some of the temples, in ancient Egypt for example, psychic training was also given to some individuals who were not mentally equipped for the rigors of occult development. A young girl so trained could be made to fall into a trance, and then could report "news" from far away. There were no electronic devices for such reporting in those days, and thus the abilities of human sensitives were used. But such sensitives were very carefully supervised and cared for, in order to preserve the accuracy of the communications and prevent "interference." They did not need to do any other kind of work or to know how to take care of themselves in any ordinary life. Now, in our present era, when an individual is a natural-born clairvoyant sensitive or medium, it is probably because he or she received this training in some past incarnation or incarnations. That is why a medium may often seem to have no particular degree of spiritual development, or even any outstanding degree of intelligence. They are often completely unable to distinguish between valid and invalid impressions in what they may receive. Their powers, which are part of what is technically called the "lower psychism," should never be mistakenly identified with the "higher psychic" powers of an individual who is "advanced," in the occult sense.

There is some talk of certain clairvoyants supposedly being able to "read the akashic records." According to the definition given by H. P. B., the Sanskrit term *akasha* means "the subtle, supersensuous spiritual essence which pervades all space. the primordial substance." It is true that this substance is supposed to retain some kind of impression of everything which occurs or has occurred. And a very highly developed individual, an adept, is indeed supposed to be able to read the akashic records and look back into past events, if he so desires, like looking at a motion picture. But this is definitely not something which is possible to an ordinary clairvoyant—the expression has been erroneously adopted.

An ordinary clairvoyant may sometimes get impressions of past (or sometimes even future) events, but these impressions come, not from the *akasha*, but from the "astral" levels. And it cannot be repeated too often that the astral world is full of thought forms which may at times correspond to some physical reality, but very often correspond only to some one's private imagination! Thus, the aspiration to be able to "see" things clairvoyantly is not worthy of any one really interested in truth. If psychic development were able to give one true or reliable information, some people might consider that the risks involved were worth taking in view of the possible achievement. But since the only achievement is access to very confused and unreliable projections of one's own subconscious mind, or other people's ideas and emotions, it should be obvious that no really sensible person will pay any attention to, or spend any effort in trying to attain, any psychic powers. As stated above, such powers may develop naturally, in the course of spiritual development, but then the higher mind is able to analyze the impressions received, and distinguish between truth and illusion.

Incidentally, it is also considered wrong to attempt to use spiritual powers for any selfish, personal, material gain. Thus those systems which promise health and wealth by the tapping of some mysterious inexhaustible source of supply may be occultly wrong and dangerous to real progress. It is quite true that correct thinking and the impression of mental images upon one's own subconscious may bring about results in the physical world, because of the telepathic links between all men at the subconscious level, and because some other person may thereby be "led" to act in a way which corresponds to the desire of the originator of the mental image. Many so-called "inspirational books" do contain many true statements and helpful ideas. But the student should be careful to check the motives in his own mind and in the mind of the author of the book too. Many such books are written merely to make money. And certainly those which promise to teach the reader how to make other people obey his will are entirely wrong, from the occult point of view.

It has been suggested that the difficulties the student encounters in deciding which teachings are likely to lead him in the right direction and which are part of the temptations of what is called "the left-hand Path," represent a modernized version of the trials and tests that a candidate for occult teaching used to have to undergo, in the days of the mystery schools. One touchstone which may be useful is to remember always that true occult teaching is never sold for gain, but rather is passed on freely by those who know a little more to those who truly aspire and who seem ready for it. The basic or elementary teaching is of course no longer truly "occult," in the real meaning of the word.

Printed books which contain such teachings, which are not "secret," obviously should be expected to have a reasonable price to cover the costs of printing. But organizations which advertise "secret" lessons, and then demand a high price for enrollment, represent nothing but trickery, and no true teaching will ever be obtained through them.

There are some organizations (which do not advertise) which do give "secret" or esoteric instructions which are part of the Wisdom. But those organizations have stringent character requirements and are careful to check the real motives and real readiness of the prospective student. And the giving out of the lessons is not dependent upon the payment of fees. Usually a student will be brought into touch with such an organization only if he has already made sufficient progress in character development to have attracted the attention of some one on the "inner planes," when circumstances will be contrived to assure him of access to any further teaching he may need. A premature personal search for secret teachings will lead the student into pseudo-occultism (or possibly even actual black magic). He has all he needs to do in trying to rid himself of the "fetters" and develop the positive characteristics required on the Path, and does not need to go hunting for things for which he is not yet ready. "When the pupil is ready, the Master appears."

The whole aim of him who treads the Occult Path is not to achieve any benefit for the personality, but rather to outgrow the identification with the separated, temporary personality, and to learn to identify himself with the spiritual Self which is truly "one with the One."

Since the Path is one of gradual, although accelerated, progress, it is divided into successive stages. Before he can achieve the first Initiation, the candidate must undergo a period of testing or probation, which is sometimes called being on the Probationary Path. It is sometimes said that this stage lasts for seven years, and elsewhere that it requires three incarnations! Probably, the time may vary greatly in different cases. During the probationary period, the aspirant is under observation by one of the Masters, and is tested by him in many ways, unknown to himself. He receives instruction during his sleep, usually from some accepted "chela" or disciple (rather than directly from the Master), and in his waking consciousness he bends every effort to purify himself and develop the character qualifications needed before he can be "accepted" by a Master.

The status of "accepted disciple" is a matter of personal relationship between the aspirant and his Master, and attaining this status is not the same thing as being ready for the First Initiation, but is usually somewhat prior to it. Just what this status involves can be known only to one who has achieved it.

In this elementary discussion, very little information can be given about initiations. The subject is a very serious one, which is often treated erroneously in pseudo-occult literature. Each initiation brings about some new kind of "awakening" of the consciousness at a higher level. This expansion of consciousness is stabilized ("fixed") by the initiation experience, and the memory is thus necessarily "brought through" into the waking consciousness. Thus, if any person begins to wonder whether perhaps he has been initiated (in the occult meaning of the term), he may be sure he has not been. No "perhaps," no shadow of doubt, would be possible about the real experience. Another point which should be mentioned here is that no true initiate ever announces his status to the world at large. Therefore the men who publicly advertise themselves as being some kind of high initiate are, to put it bluntly, nothing but cheats. The whole subject is most profoundly sacred, and therefore secret.

A man who has successfully passed all the great initiations up through the Fifth, and thus become an "adept," may choose to become a Master and continue to live on earth in order to help and teach his younger brothers. There are said to be several initiations even beyond the Fifth, for some few individuals who remain connected with earth in order to serve in the higher ranks of the Occult Hierarchy, in its task of service and guidance to humanity.

In one sense, the Head of the Hierarchy may be considered to be the Bodhisattva, or Buddha-to-be. But the terms "Manu" and "Mahachohan" are used for two others supposed to be of equal rank with Him. The Bodhisattva is said to be upon the "Ray" of Love-Wisdom, the Manu upon the "Ray" of Will or Power, and the Mahachohan upon the "Ray" of Activity. Other terms are sometimes used, and the subject of the "Rays" is quite beyond the competence of the present writer. One finds reference also, sometimes, to a mysterious being called the "One Initiator." The Bodhisattva, Manu, and Mahachohan, in any given era, are said to be the highest of those who have evolved from our own humanity, yet still refrain from entering Nirvana. But the "One Initiator" is sometimes referred to as the "spirit" of the whole planet, the globe itself being his only physical vehicle. All of these things are far too "occult" to be really understood by anyone not "initiated," but the student may come across references to them.

The Path involves unceasing, strenuous effort, and the willing sacrifice of all that the lower self holds dear. But, in compensation, he who treads it comes to identify himself with his higher Self, and he gains also the indescribable joy of the conciousness of the companionship of the Great Ones—the joy of adding his little ability to theirs in the work of accelerating the progress of the great Plan.